Empowering Readers

Empowering Readers

Integrated Strategies to Comprehend Expository Texts

Mary L. Hoch and Jana L. McNally

ROWMAN & LITTLEFIELD
Lanham • Boulder • New York • London

Published by Rowman & Littlefield
An imprint of The Rowman & Littlefield Publishing Group, Inc.
4501 Forbes Boulevard, Suite 200, Lanham, Maryland 20706
www.rowman.com

6 Tinworth Street, London SE11 5AL, United Kingdom

Copyright © 2020 by Mary L. Hoch and Jana L. McNally

All rights reserved. No part of this book may be reproduced in any form or by any electronic or mechanical means, including information storage and retrieval systems, without written permission from the publisher, except by a reviewer who may quote passages in a review.

British Library Cataloguing in Publication Information Available

Library of Congress Cataloging-in-Publication Data
Names: Hoch, Mary L., author | McNally, Jana L., author.
Title: Empowering Readers : integrated strategies to comprehend expository texts / Mary L. Hoch and Jana L. McNally.
Description: Lanham, Maryland : Rowman & Littlefield, 2019. | Includes bibliographical references and index.
Identifiers: LCCN 2019040036 (print) | LCCN 2019040037 (ebook) | ISBN 9781475851229 (cloth) | ISBN 9781475851236 (paperback) | ISBN 9781475851243 (epub)
Subjects: LCSH: Reading comprehension—Study and teaching (Elementary) | Exposition (Rhetoric)—Study and teaching (Elementary)
Classification: LCC LB1573.7 .H64 2019 (print) | LCC LB1573.7 (ebook) | DDC 372.47—dc23
LC record available at https://lccn.loc.gov/2019040036
LC ebook record available at https://lccn.loc.gov/2019040037

Contents

Foreword		vii
Acknowledgments		ix
An Introduction to Integrated Strategies		xi
1	*Before, During,* and *After* Reading	1
2	Teaching Text Structure	15
3	Using Assessment to Drive the Process	23
4	Description	31
5	Problem and Solution	39
6	Sequence	47
7	Compare and Contrast	57
8	Cause and Effect	69
	Closing Thoughts	77
Appendix A		79
Appendix B		85
Appendix C		91
References		93
Index		95
About the Authors		101

Foreword

Every so often, in education as in other fields, someone combines some "old" ideas to create something new which is both exciting and innovative. This is what Hoch and McNally have done in this book. By combining and adapting some familiar ideas, the authors bring a new look to a process of integrating strategies for reading and learning in a carefully structured approach for both teachers and students. As a classroom teacher, I was always happy to have a structure and routines for my lessons (as were my students), and the authors provide these in spades through the use of graphic organizers and excellent classroom examples. Their experience of working with teachers and students is apparent, not just from the examples but from the anecdotes that make the book both readable and enjoyable. In addition, they answer questions that teachers commonly ask about helping students learn from expository text, not least of which is a full chapter on assessment. I became interested and willing to learn from the opening paragraphs of the introduction and remained so throughout the book. Each chapter provided something new but was grounded in theory and practice, so that at the end I felt confident that I could try these ideas with students. I commend Hoch and McNally for providing us all with an excellent resource to improve our teaching of reading.

Peter Fisher
Coauthor *Teaching Vocabulary in All Classrooms*
and *Teaching Academic Vocabulary, K-8*

Acknowledgments

While supervising a summer reading clinic for our graduate students, we saw firsthand the struggles teachers and students faced in dealing with the complexities of informational text. We realized that there was a plethora of strategies already in existence but wanted to create a method that tied together many strategies, across all phases of reading, and was easily adaptable for all the grade levels we worked with. This was much easier said than done! This book pushed our thinking and forced us to dig deeply into the intricacies of what it means to comprehend.

We are grateful to all the teachers who were willing to work with us and put our thinking into practice. We appreciate their openness to try something new, allow us to see it in action, and provide honest feedback, which helped immensely in guiding our thinking. We offer our profound thanks to Adam and Michelle, who went above and beyond to host our ideas in their classrooms. Their dedication to teaching and learning is admirable. We also thank one of our mentors, Peter Fisher, who graciously provided us with feedback and insights. And, last, but certainly not least, we thank our families for supporting us every step of the way. Tim, Wilk, Theo, John, Mason, Bailey, and Max—we are beyond blessed to have these amazing guys rooting us on!

An Introduction to Integrated Strategies

On a dreary spring day in the Chicago suburbs, we visited Ellen Page's fourth-grade classroom. Spring break was one week away and yet the weather still gave the impression of winter. The kids were restless. The teachers were restless.

During this visit, Jana and Mary expected to observe the students engaging with various expository texts about ancient Egypt. At the last minute, the teacher instead read aloud a fictional picture book with an ancient Egyptian setting. When the class was over, they asked Ellen about the last-minute switch.

"Honestly," she said, "these kids are so checked out. I just wanted to engage them."

Mary was surprised. "The articles you sent me were engaging! I especially thought the one about the tools they used to mummify bodies would have been a hit. I mean . . . pulling brain matter out through the nose . . . yikes!"

"Well . . .," Ellen started slowly, "with the picture book, we can talk about the characters and the plot twists. Reading expository text is different. It's . . .," she trailed off.

Ellen couldn't quite verbalize her reluctance to use expository text. This is a feeling Jana could connect with. When she was a brand-new seventh-grade language arts teacher, if she had a choice of materials, she chose a fictional story over an expository text every time.

Many teachers have shared with us this same preference for fictional stories. However, the recent focus on the importance of expository text at all grade levels has certainly changed this practice. Along with this change, many teachers are discovering a newfound love for nonfiction. The quantity and quality of expository books and articles available for students of all ages is at an all-time high. But implementing expository text in the classroom is not the same as implementing fictional stories. Along with a renewed focus on expository text comes a renewed set of challenges.

Reading new information is one way people learn. It is no secret that the skills necessary for understanding information in text commonly referred to as *expository* are different from the skills used when reading literary materials. The way text is structured is one aspect of expository text that separates it from literary text. This can contribute to the challenges many students face in trying to construct meaning while reading to learn.

In this book, we present an integrated strategy approach that can be used to accompany text structure instruction on the five most commonly used expository text structures: *compare and contrast, cause and effect, problem and solution, description,* and *sequence*. Within this strategy, we designed a method for using keywords in a way that helps students think about the structure of the text. However, we did not stop there. In helping readers to develop higher-level understanding with challenging materials, we also felt it was important to integrate other essential reading comprehension components that foster understanding. Therefore, we use *predicting* and *summarizing* in a way that ties together text structure and word knowledge of keywords. Structure Sorts follow a strategic four-step process that guides students before reading (*Sort and Predict*), during reading (*Read and Check*), and after reading (*Summarize*).

The approach to teaching and learning presented in this book is based on the premise that meaning is constructed through active engagement with the text during all three phases of reading. In addition, social interactions between the teacher and the students as well as student to student are the cornerstones on which meaning is made, checked, and extended.

Helping students understand how authors structure text in a way that fosters understanding is well documented. For example, Meyer's (1975, 1979) early research identified the most common organizational patterns for presenting information in expository texts. The five text structures that are most often identified are *compare and contrast, cause and effect, problem and solution, description,* and *sequence*. Teaching text structure as a means for identifying organizational patterns can help readers classify information so that it can be used to assist with recall and overall comprehension (Kintsch, 1974; Meyer, 1975; Meyer, Brandt, & Bluth, 1980).

For more than forty years, continued research on this topic has deemed it effective in improving comprehension of expository texts (Armbruster, Anderson, & Ostertag, 1987; Englert & Hiebert, 1984; Hall, Sabey, & McClellan, 2005; Meyer, 1987; Richgels et al., 1987). In a recent meta-analysis of forty-five studies, Hebert et al. (2016) sought to determine the impact of text structure instruction on student comprehension of expository texts. They found that teaching text structures improved student comprehension of expository text and that knowledge about text structures can be transferred across contexts.

Although many instructional strategies have been introduced for helping students learn to identify the structures used in expository texts (e.g., Roehling et al., 2017), our work with teachers has led us to believe that this is an extremely challenging concept which should begin in the primary grades. Although we believe this to be the case, teaching text structures as a means for gaining understanding poses many challenges for all students, and even more so for our younger learners.

To begin, the ability to organize information while reading requires a level of mental capacity that may not yet be developed in primary grades (Englert & Hiebert, 1984). Therefore, scaffolds that guide students in their thinking about the structure of the text may be necessary. For example, we have long known that students benefit from the use of graphic organizers, which helps students organize and recall information from expository texts (e.g., Alvermann, 1981).

Furthermore, other characteristics of expository text exist that add to the complex nature of reading to learn. One such characteristic is the high-level or technical vocabulary that is usually embedded in expository text. According to Blachowicz et al. (2013), students need opportunities to learn new words in text and opportunities to speak and write about them.

Beck, McKeown, and Kucan (2013) identify three tiers of words and argue that the focus for teachers should be on teaching words in tier 2. Tier 1 words are the most basic and should not need to be taught in school. Tier 2 words are high utility and transferable across domains. Tier 3 is made up of low-frequency words that are specific to a particular domain. Using Beck, McKeown, and Kucan's three-tiered approach (2013), it is important for teachers to consider how the words of any given passage impact text complexity.

Thus, it was our goal to develop an integrated strategy approach to help teachers scaffold text structure instruction in a way that attends to the developing mental capacity of students, while also teaching keywords from tiers 2 and 3 (Beck, McKeown, & Kucan, 2013) that often make reading to learn more challenging. Our definition of an integrated strategy approach is embedding multiple reading strategies before, during, and after reading to empower students to make connections and build comprehension at all stages of reading.

The chapters of this book will guide you through the implementation of the Structure Sort process. In chapter 1, we begin with an in-depth look at the processes we want to teach our readers to engage in *before*, *during*, and *after* reading. In chapter 2, we point out the connection between teaching text structures and the Structure Sort method. In chapter 3, we discuss practical methods of formatively assessing students work. Then, in chapters 4 to 8 we describe how to use the Structure Sort method with each of the five traditional text structures. For each, we begin by discussing the text structure and how and why authors use it in expository writing. We then guide you through the Structure Sort process. We provide classroom examples and a step-by-step approach to implementation to help you get a feel for what it looks like with each text structure, during all three phases of reading. The book concludes with our closing thoughts.

Whether you are beginning or continuing your journey with reading to learn, we hope Structure Sorts will serve as a framework that will empower your students to develop the mental capacity needed to build comprehension and become critical thinkers.

Chapter 1

Before, During, and *After* Reading

> **CHAPTER FOCUS: In this chapter we will focus on teacher preparation and what to expect during each phase of the reading process.**

As a child in elementary school, Jana remembers telling her parents one year that her least favorite subject in school was literature.

"But you love to read!" her mother argued.

"But literature class isn't where we read," she said matter-of-factly. "It's where we have to find answers."

In sharing this story with undergraduate education majors, it is clear that this experience is not uncommon. For many students reading class is all about what happens after the text is read:

- Can you answer the following ten questions *after* reading this poem?
- Can you give a report *after* reading this novel?
- Can you take a test *after* reading this chapter in your textbook?

There is so much emphasis placed upon what happens after reading that many students, Jana included, learn to skip the reading altogether and instead work on the end product by skimming the text (or the Internet) for answers.

As a first-year teacher, Jana cringes to remember that she started the year teaching with a similar focus on what students could complete *after* reading. Fortunately, midway through her first year as a teacher, she was introduced to the powerful research on the importance of explicit instruction in reading strategies *before, during,* and *after* reading, especially with content-area text (e.g., National Reading Panel 2000; Vacca, Vacca & Mraz 2011).

Once teachers begin the implementation of strategies at all three phases of reading, many report an immediate change not only in the ability but also in the attitude of their students. Students are eager to begin reading, are more engaged with the text during reading, and produce higher-level products after reading. The use of strategies before, during, and after reading is a widely written about, demonstrated, and used practice in schools (e.g., Blachowicz & Ogle, 2008; Harvey & Goudvis, 2017). However, the most common frustrations we hear from teachers and teacher candidates about using strategies during the three phases of reading, especially with expository text include the following:

- *How do I know which strategy to use for which text?*
- *Finding three different strategies for each phase of reading for each new text we read is overwhelming to me.*
- *Giving my students so many strategies at all times is overwhelming to them.*

With Structure Sorts, we aim to streamline the strategy process for teachers by covering all three phases of reading with one approach. In addition, each sort directly corresponds to the five most commonly used text structures so there is no guessing which strategies will work best with which texts.

In this chapter, we will describe the step-by-step processes we want to teach readers to engage in during every phase of reading. We describe what should occur before, during, and after reading, and how the teacher should prepare for each step.

PREPARING FOR STRUCTURE SORTS

One afternoon, as Jana was getting ready to begin one of her content-area methods courses, one of her brightest undergraduate students came rushing up at her with a look of panic.

"Dr. McNally, I don't think I can teach this Social Studies lesson to my second graders tomorrow."

Jana was surprised, considering the student had spent hours organizing, planning, and refining this lesson. It was inquiry-based, used cooperative learning groups, and included a variety of texts at differentiated levels. It was, simply, one of the best lesson plans she had reviewed that semester.

He continued, "The problem is the students are doing all of the work. They are the ones reading. They are the ones researching. They are the ones finding the evidence. They are the ones reporting the information. What am I doing?"

He failed to recognize that everything he had done to prepare them for the reading (introducing vocabulary, building background knowledge, and discussing the text structure) counted as "teaching."

We can think of no better use of classroom time than to have prepared your students so well for the reading that they are now "doing all the work."

This is why we have always found the *before* phase of reading to be the most important.

Before students read expository text, a classroom teacher should aim to:

- choose a text or chunk of text that is at an appropriate level and of manageable length;
- identify the text structure and features;
- set a purpose for reading;
- identify new or difficult vocabulary (tier 2 and tier 3); and
- activate prior knowledge and build background knowledge.

Each of these components will front-load instruction before reading to assist all readers in tackling the demands of difficult expository text. Some advanced preparation on the part of the teacher is required for each.

Choose a Text

To prepare for using a Structure Sort, the classroom teacher will first want to choose a text or chunk of text that is short enough for the students to tackle without becoming frustrated but long enough to convey the concept or topic in a way that extends their thinking. The length of the text will be highly dependent on the grade level of the students. For example, in second grade, the teacher may want to begin with a text that is between 200 and 300 words, whereas, in fourth grade, 400 to 500 words might be a good starting point. It is better to start with shorter text and gradually increase the length and level. Structure Sorts can also be used with chapters of content-area texts, such as science or social studies. When doing so, however, we caution teachers to start with only a chunk of text or one section of a chapter. Some great online resources for short, leveled expository texts can be found in table 1.1.

Table 1.1. Online Expository Article Resources.

Dogo News: www.dogonews.com
Free informational articles for grades 3–8

Time for Kids: www.timeforkids.com/news
Free articles on current events archived by date and subject categories

Smithsonian Tween Tribune: www.tweentribune.com
Free articles on current events available in four Lexile levels and by grade

ReadWorks: https://www.readworks.org/
Free leveled reading passages in various subjects

News ELA: www.newsela.com
Free articles on current events available in four Lexile levels

Identify the Structure

Next, the teacher will need to determine the structure of the expository text. Our approach addresses the five most commonly used and taught structures in elementary school: *compare and contrast, cause and effect, problem and solution, description,* and *sequence*. Determining the structure of the text in advance is often the most challenging step of this approach. Although there are often signal words that can assist teachers in determining the text structure (see table 1.2), not all authors write their texts using perfectly predictable patterns. Therefore, if a text structure is not initially obvious, a teacher should determine the most important idea(s) from the text. Within those ideas, the teacher should look for signal words and patterns to find the best fit. Keep in mind that authors often incorporate more than one structure in any given text. When determining text structure, it is important to look at the overall macrostructure, rather than considering microstructures that may exist at the paragraph level.

Set the Purpose

Once the text structure has been identified, the teacher should determine the purpose of the text. What information do they want their students to gain from this text? From those key ideas, the teacher should select important tier 2 or tier 3 keywords. It is important to include words from both tiers for content learning to occur (Blachowicz et al., 2013).

Choose Keywords

Choosing keywords is the most important part of preparing for the Structure Sort, as the words chosen are essential to every step in the Structure Sort

Table 1.2. Text Structure Signal Words.

Compare and contrast	*Cause and effect*	*Problem and solution*	*Description*	*Sequence*
However	Because	Problem	Like	First
Similarly	Therefore	The question is	For example	Next
Either . . . or	If . . . then	A solution is	Also	Then
Different from	Thus	One answer is	To illustrate	Before
Same as	This led to . . .	–	In addition	After
As opposed to	Since	–	Another	Not long after
Instead of	In order to	–	Furthermore	Initially
As well as	Yet	–	To begin with	–
But	For this reason	–	Such as	–
On the other hand	As a result of	–	–	–

process. They will be used to activate prior knowledge and help the students begin building background about the topic. The words will be used to assist students in generating a prediction before reading. In addition, they will be used after reading to write a summary of key ideas.

If a teacher only selects difficult or new vocabulary that is unrelated to the important concepts, the student's prediction may not be adequate and the summary writing will be a challenge. Therefore, a teacher may want to work backward (summary first, then pull out the keywords) to ensure the words selected will assist students in comprehension, purpose, prediction, and summary writing.

Depending on the length of the text, the teacher will select between four and six keywords directly related to the purpose and structure of the text (the connection between keywords and text structure will be further explained in subsequent chapters specific to the text structures). In addition, the teacher should also select two to three new or difficult vocabulary words that students will encounter in the text, for a total of six to nine keywords. Age of students, text length and difficulty, and topic will certainly impact the number of words selected, but it is not recommended that teachers select more than ten words, as too many words may lead to a superficial understanding.

Prepare the Graphic Organizer

The graphic organizers for all five Structure Sort types can be found in Appendix A. To prepare for the Structure Sort, a classroom teacher will enter both the title and the keywords on the Structure Sort Graphic Organizer. Older students have the option of entering the title and words themselves. Once the Structure Sort Graphic Organizer is prepared, students begin the process of sorting based on text structure.

To illustrate this process for you, we will walk you through a sample Structure Sort prepared by fifth-grade teacher Bonnie Drewes for her students' work with a descriptive text about ice castles. You can see her prepared Structure Sort in figure 1.1.

Before continuing to the *before* reading portion of this chapter, we share a summary of the preparation required by the teacher in preparing for Structure Sorts:

- Determine the structure of the expository text selection.
- Identify the purpose for reading.
- Select six to nine keywords from the text directly related to the purpose and key ideas or concepts.

To help you get accustomed to preparing for a Structure Sort, we have included several samples of graphic organizers that have been prepared for each text structure using the online resources we provided in this chapter. These can be found in Appendix B.

STRUCTURE SORT: Description

TEXT TITLE: Ice Castle Magic

KEY WORDS: structures, formation, icicle, frigid, carve, conditions, construct, metamorphosis

- **SORT**

MAIN IDEA	+ or -	DETAIL	+ or -

- **PREDICT** _____

_____

_____

- **READ & CHECK (+ or -)**

- **SUMMARIZE** _____

_____

_____

_____

Figure 1.1. Teacher-Prepared Structure Sort Sample. *Source*: Jana McNally.

BEFORE READING

Once students are given the prepared Structure Sort (which includes the title and keywords), the first step for students is to sort words based on where they *predict* they will be categorized in the text. For example, in a Structure Sort about ice castles, students would look at a keyword, such as *icicle*, and decide if they think *icicle* would be part of the main idea or the detail. The key here is for students to be thinking about both the keywords and how those words may fit into the specific text structure.

It is recommended that the teacher read each keyword out loud while students sort the words. Hearing the word orally helps students make sense of the words they see in print. The sorting can be done in a variety of ways:

- Students independently sort the keywords into categories.
- Students work in partners or small groups to sort the words together.

Once the words are sorted, it is critical that students have time to verbally discuss the "why" behind their decisions. Why did they decide to place a certain word in a certain category? This can be done in small groups or with the whole class. This is an essential step in the *Before Reading* process because it facilitates critical thinking discussions among students to make arguments for why certain words belong in certain categories. We want to stress that it is not important *where* they place their words but rather that they can explain the thinking process for *why* they placed their words in each category.

After sorting the words, students will write a one-sentence prediction of what they think the text will be about using both the keywords and their knowledge of the text structure. Students should be encouraged to use as many of the keywords as they can in their prediction. After writing their predictions, students should be given time to verbally share their predictions in partners, small groups, or with the whole class. In continuing with the previous Structure Sort example, a sample of one of Bonnie's student's sorts and prediction can be seen in figure 1.2.

Once students have completed their sorting and prediction, the teacher will then share their purpose for the *during* reading portion of the text. Before continuing to the *during* reading portion of this chapter, we share a summary of students' objectives for the *before* reading component:

- Read through the keywords and sort them into the categories based on where they *predict* they will fall in the text.
- Discuss the *why* behind their word placement.
- Write a brief prediction of what they think the text will be about using both the keywords and their knowledge of the text structure.

Chapter 1

STRUCTURE SORT: Description

TEXT TITLE: *Ice Castle Magic*

KEY WORDS: structures, formation, icicle, frigid, carve, conditions, construct, metamorphosis

- **SORT**

MAIN IDEA	+ or -	DETAIL	+ or -
icicle		formation	
metamorphosis		frigid	
structure		conditions	
carve		construct	

- **PREDICT** Icicles are carved into a structure to form ice castles like in frozen movie!

- **READ & CHECK (+ or -)**

- **SUMMARIZE** _____

Figure 1.2. "Before Reading" Structure Sort Sample. *Source*: Jana McNally.

DURING READING

Often, when a person reads a piece of text they are not particularly interested in, they will find themselves nearing the end of the text and thinking, "I have absolutely no idea what I just read." When we describe this sensation to undergraduate students, nearly all of them nod and smile as we are describing something they have all experienced. When we ask them what type of text they are reading, nine times out of ten it is an expository piece. To avoid this troublesome reading practice, while students are reading an expository text, it is important for them to

- stay engaged with the text as an active reader,
- monitor their own comprehension, and
- process what is being read.

The Read and Check component of the Structure Sort enables students to do all three.

As students read the text, each time they come across one of the keywords, they will stop and check to see if they agree or disagree with where they sorted the word. Continuing with the earlier ice castle example, if a student sorted the word *icicle* into the Main Idea category, they would then decide if they still agree that the word *icicle* is part of the main idea. If they agree, they should put a plus (+) sign on the graphic organizer next to the word. If they instead think *icicle* should have been part of the detail, they would put a minus (-) next to the word.

This system builds in a minimum of six stopping points for students throughout the reading. Not only are they stopping when they come to the word, but they are also thinking about how the word relates to the text structure and the main idea. Stopping and thinking gives students a chance to monitor their own comprehension throughout the text so that they do not get to the end and wonder "what did I just read?" It also allows students to process the text as they begin to make sense of how these keywords relate to the main idea. Finally, students, especially primary students, are eager to find out if their predictions were correct. This gives them motivation as they read to keep them engaged with the text. A sample of Bonnie's students' continuing work with the Structure Sort can be seen in figure 1.3.

Using the plus (+) and minus (−) system rather than erasing and rewriting their word in the new category is helpful for two reasons. First, it can be done in a second, which allows students to focus on reading and thinking rather than writing. Second, it gives students and the teacher a way to keep track of their original thinking and predictions which gives insight into each student's background knowledge on both the topic and the text structure.

Like the *before* reading stage, there are several ways a classroom teacher can implement the *during* reading component:

- Students independently read and check the keywords.
- Students read out loud with partners or small groups and check the words together.
- Students read and check independently first and then discuss with partners/small groups/the whole class to determine a plus or minus based on majority decisions.

STRUCTURE SORT: Description

TEXT TITLE: Ice Castle Magic

KEY WORDS: structures, formation, icicle, frigid, carve, conditions, construct, metamorphosis

- **SORT**

MAIN IDEA	+ or -	DETAIL	+ or -
icicle	−	formation	+
metamorphosis	−	frigid	+
structure	+	conditions	+
carve	+	construct	−

- **PREDICT** Icicles are carved into a structure to form ice castles like in frozen movie!

- **READ & CHECK** (+ or -)

- **SUMMARIZE**

Figure 1.3. "During Reading" Structure Sort Sample. *Source*: Jana McNally.

Once again, the third option is an extra step and requires additional time but facilitates critical thinking discussions among students to make arguments for why certain words belong in certain categories. When first introducing Structure Sorts, a classroom teacher may want to use the second option (partners/small groups) as a scaffold for students. Or, with emergent readers, a teacher may choose to read the entire text aloud to their class and discuss the words as a whole group. However, teachers should eventually aim to regularly implement this using independent reading. It is critical that students have the opportunity to independently read complex texts. The Structure Sort gives students a support to facilitate independent reading with built-in stopping points to monitor comprehension and process what they are reading.

Before continuing to the *after* reading portion of this chapter, we share a summary of student objectives for the *during* reading component:

- Read the text and stop at each of the keywords.
- Decide if they agree or disagree with their predicted categorization of the keywords by placing a plus (+) or minus (−) next to each keyword.

AFTER READING

Often, when a parent finishes reading a book to a toddler, the child will chuck it to the floor and instantly thrust a new book in their face. There is literally a one-second lag between finishing one book and starting the next.

Unfortunately, for many teachers, this practice can feel familiar as they rush to finish, for example, one chapter of social studies and immediately move on to the next one to keep up with their curriculum pacing chart. This "rush" to power through text is one of the most frequent complaints we hear from classroom teachers, and frankly, we find it to be one of the most damaging practices happening in schools. Imagine training months for a marathon, keeping your focus through the whole 26.2 miles, and then right as your cross the finish line you are to immediately get in your car, go home, and begin training for a bike race. After all of the mental and physical preparation and focus during the race, you would completely miss the rewards of celebrating with other runners and the much-needed physical component of cooling down, eating a snack, stretching, and the like. We cannot imagine one would ever want to run a marathon again.

Similarly, if ample time is not given to the *after* reading component, students miss the chance to feel rewarded and build their mental capacity for understanding text. After devoting so much preparation to *before* and *during* reading practices, the *after* reading component is a chance to see the fruits of your labor and assess how far your students have advanced in their comprehension. After reading expository text, students can build their comprehension by

- summarizing what was read,
- elaborating on their understanding of the text, and
- applying their new knowledge.

Before students can elaborate and apply, the first step is to summarize what was read. Structure Sorts lead students through this process with the final "Summarize" step. Here, students create a summary of the text using as many of the keywords as possible. Having the keywords already in front of them aids the students with the summary writing process. In addition, students have

---

STRUCTURE SORT: Description

TEXT TITLE: Ice Castle Magic

KEY WORDS: structures, formation, icicle, frigid, carve, conditions, construct, metamorphosis

- **SORT**

MAIN IDEA	+ or -	DETAIL	+ or -
icicle	−	formation	+
metamorphosis	−	frigid	+
structure	+	conditions	+
carve	+	construct	−

- **PREDICT** Icicles are carved into a structure to form ice castles like in frozen movie!

_____

_____

- **READ & CHECK** (+ or -)

- **SUMMARIZE** People construct ice castles by carving into ice structures. They need frigid conditions or the castle could go through a metamorphosis and change formation!

Figure 1.4. "After Reading" Structure Sort Sample. *Source*: Jana McNally.

Table 1.3. Structure Sort Summary Chart.

Preparation
- Determine the structure of the expository text selection.
- Identify the purpose for reading.
- Select six to nine keywords from the text directly related to the purpose and key ideas or concepts.

Before
- Read through the keywords and sort them into the categories based on where they *predict* they will fall in the text.
- Write a brief prediction of what they think the text will be about using both the keywords and their knowledge of the text structure.

During
- Read the text and stop at each of the keywords.
- Decide if they agree or disagree with their predicted categorization of the keywords using a plus or minus next to each keyword.

After
- Summarize what was read using as many keywords as possible.

---

their original prediction written on the Structure Sort. This allows them to check and confirm, revise, and extend their original thinking. The completed Structure Sort example can be seen in figure 1.4.

By the time students have completed this final step, they will have immersed themselves in rich thinking and conversation about the content, had multiple opportunities to use vocabulary in an authentic situation, used the predicting strategy to activate prior knowledge and build comprehension, written two brief expository pieces of text, and evaluated their own thinking. This is what sets Structure Sorts apart from the multitude of nonfiction strategies permeating schools. And the end result is students who feel empowered and engaged in expository text.

During this chapter, we walked you through the teacher preparation phase, as well as the students' Structure Sort journey in the *before*, *during*, and *after* reading phases. This is summarized in table 1.3. You will also find a Quick Steps—Implementation Guide in Appendix C to help you get started.

In the chapters ahead, we provide you with specific information about each text structure and text samples similar to those you might find in the resources found in table 1.1 as well as helpful hints, troubleshooting tips, and classroom examples to illustrate the power of Structure Sorts in everyday classroom use.

Key Points

- Front-loading instruction before students encounter a difficult text helps to build independent readers.
- Determination of text structure can be tricky even for teachers. Look at both purpose and macrostructure to help make your determination.

- When selecting keywords, focus on tier 2 words as well as words that are necessary for summarizing the text.
- Allow ample time for students to share the why behind their word placement. It does not matter if they correctly predict the categories for their words. What matters is that they can explain why they chose to place each word in its specific category.
- Give students time to share their predictions as a way to build keyword knowledge and engagement.
- Encourage students to use the "Read and Check" portion as a way to self-monitor their comprehension.
- Don't rush through the after portion summary writing. Give students time to share, elaborate, and celebrate their success with text.

Chapter 2

Teaching Text Structure

> **CHAPTER FOCUS: In this chapter we point out the relationship that exists between text structure instruction and the Structure Sort process, and how it leads to deepened understanding.**

Now that you've had a glimpse into the Structure Sort process, let's pause and consider how this process fits with text structure instruction and facilitates reading comprehension. The relationship between text structure instruction and the Structure Sort process is symbiotic. The goal of teaching text structure strategies is to help students use the way in which the author has organized the text to organize their own understanding (Meyer, Brandt, & Bluth, 1980). This organization helps the reader to identify and think about relationships communicated by the text, which, ultimately, aids in comprehension (Meyer & Ray, 2011). Eventually, we want students to be able to use such structures and logic to organize their own writing. Thus, instruction on all five text structures is a necessary and vital component of the Structure Sort process. And, Structure Sorts help readers get to the heart of understanding in a way that is not possible with text structure instruction alone. In this way, an interdependent relationship exists between text structure instruction and the Structure Sort process.

TEACHER DECISION-MAKING

During our text structure work with teachers, we are frequently asked the following questions:

How do you introduce each text structure?
Is there a specific order we should use when introducing the different structures?
How long do you spend on each structure?

Unfortunately, there are no easy answers to these questions. So let's start with what we do *not* recommend.

We do not recommend doing a "text structure of the month." This feels inauthentic and unnatural. It also makes each structure feel disconnected from the other structures and students will not learn how to identify and recognize structures on their own. For example, if students spend the whole month of October working with only the cause and effect structure, then they can anticipate that any expository text they receive that month will be a cause and effect structure. Then, when they move to the sequence text structure in November, they will know each text is structured sequentially, without even considering the cause and effect structure they learned the previous month. This does not prepare students to identify text structure features on a daily basis in authentic reading situations.

Similarly, we also do not recommend having a prescribed order and length for each structure. Prescribing, for example, "two weeks per text structure for the first ten weeks of school" does not take into account student needs, interest, or connection to the curriculum.

Instead, we recommend starting the year by introducing students to all five text structures at the same time. Then, as the year progresses, your texts and curriculum dictate your Structure Sorts. For example, if your third-grade students are in the middle of a unit on animals, then you may have a variety of expository articles on animals. Some articles may be descriptive, some sequential, and some compare and contrast. Thus, you would focus on those three text structures during your unit. Then, as you move on to your next curriculum unit, you will once again use the texts and topics to determine which text structures are your focus.

But how do you introduce five text structures at once? There are many ways to do this, and we imagine you may already have a tried-and-true method for this introduction. But in case you are looking for inspiration, we will walk you through some sample lessons from two teachers. First, we will look at Joan's fourth-grade classroom as she introduces text structure to her students. Then, we will step inside Sarah's fifth-grade classroom where she provides additional explicit instruction and text structure support for her students.

JOAN'S ANCHOR LESSONS

Joan William's fourth-grade classroom is always noisy and she wouldn't have it any other way. Students are seated four to a table with a small supply center of pencils, pens, paper, Kleenex, hand sanitizer, scissors, and the like at the center of each table. Her students have been practicing working together in cooperative groups for the first three weeks of school and Joan is pleased with their progress. In the coming weeks they will be reading *Bud, Not Buddy* (Curtis 1999), a novel about an African American boy who searches for his father during the Great Depression. During this unit, students will be reading expository text about related topics such as the Great Depression, Civil Rights, and orphanages in the 1920s. For her first anchor lesson on text structure, Joan has selected five short expository articles about the Great Depression. Each article is written using a different text structure, although she has not informed the students of this yet. These articles include:

"What Caused the Crash?" (cause and effect)
"Recession vs. Depression" (compare and contrast)
"If You Lived in 1929" (description)
"A Brief History of Black Friday" (sequence)
"Surviving the Great Depression" (problem and solution)

A set of each of these articles was given to each table of students. Joan selected the first article—"What Caused the Crash?"—and modeled reading aloud the text. When she finished, she modeled a "think aloud" to show students what she noticed about the text structure of the article. For example, she noted the article listed several potential reasons (causes) for the Great Depression. On an anchor chart, she listed her findings about the text structure of this article. She not only did most of the sharing but also encouraged students to add their ideas as well. Students then paired off at their tables and partner read two of the remaining four articles taking notes on the text structure the same way their teacher had. They then shared their findings with the other students at their table.

The next day, students revisited the articles and shared their findings as a whole class. Once again, Joan used an anchor chart for each article to make notes of the students' text structure findings. If students missed something she felt was important, she modeled her thinking about the structure to add her own findings to the anchor chart (see figure 2.1).

On the third day, Joan pulled out the anchor charts and the articles once again. She gave each table five Post-it Notes with one of the five text structures written on each note. As a table, students worked together to place the name of the text structure (i.e., description) on the article they felt it

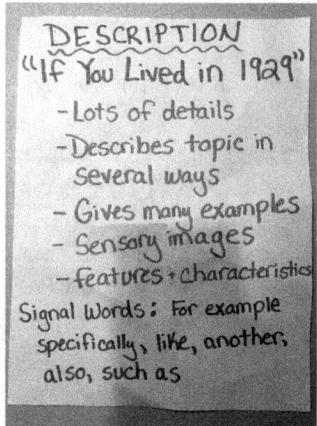

Figure 2.1. Description Anchor Chart. *Source*: Jana McNally.

corresponded with. Students were encouraged to explicitly state the *why* when deciding on which text structure matched which article. Once tables had come to an agreement, they shared their ideas as a whole class. As the class determined which article matched which text structure, Joan added headings to the anchor charts with the names of the text structure as the title (see figure 2.1). She also shared further information about each text structure including the common signal words. As she shared, students went back to the articles to search for these signal words.

These anchor charts would remain on display in the coming weeks as Joan continually made reference to them as students came across new pieces of expository text. By no means are students "done" learning about text structure, but these three anchor lessons laid the foundation for students to begin recognizing the structures they will encounter on a daily basis. Having this foundation underway, Joan is ready to introduce Structure Sorts.

SARAH'S EXPLICIT INSTRUCTION

Although we recommend introducing students to all five text structures early on and simultaneously, we realize that sometimes additional explicit instruction and scaffolding is required. If students seem to be struggling with grasping an understanding of one or more text structures, then additional instructional support is needed.

It's late September, as we step inside Sarah Bruce's fifth-grade classroom. Since the start of the school year, Sarah has been integrating informational reading and writing into her literacy curriculum. She has already introduced all five text structures to her students but has noticed their struggle with the descriptive text structure. Particularly, they struggled with honing in on the main idea and how it differs from supporting details. She also anticipated a lot of descriptive text in the unit on animals they recently started, and so she decided to spend some more time on this structure before introducing Structure Sorts. Her goals were to facilitate an understanding of the genre and topic, and to have her students use this structure for descriptive writing.

Sarah started by planning several mini-lessons over the course of a week on using keywords to find the main idea of a text. To begin, Sarah chose a short text that would provide topical knowledge for an animal research project they recently started. The subject they were researching was how animals adapt to their environment, and this short piece of text focused on birds. The text was also clearly organized as description.

Sarah introduced an anchor chart she created, which contained three prompts:

1. What is the author's main idea?
2. How do you know?
3. What information does the author give to support this idea?

She displayed the text for the students to see and read it aloud:

Birds inhabit most of the earth. Each habitat poses unique challenges that birds must face. They need to adapt in order to survive. One of the most challenging places on earth for birds is the ocean. Some birds living near the ocean spend most of their lives in flight. As such, birds like the wandering albatross, have vast wingspans to make flight effortless. Others must adapt to freezing ocean water. Penguins have thick layers of waterproof feathers to help them survive freezing ocean conditions. Adaptations such as these have made it possible for birds to live almost anywhere.

Sarah referred to the anchor chart. She explained that authors use this text structure to provide readers with information about one or more ideas. However, she explained, sifting through a lot of information can be difficult. The text's structure can be used to provide the readers with clues that help in determining what is important.

She then introduced words that help the readers in identifying the structure as description. She listed them on the anchor chart: *one reason, for example, like, also, to illustrate, in addition, another, furthermore, to begin with, such as* (see figure 2.2).

She explained that these words are used because they help the author explain their main idea and signal to the reader that more information is coming. Sarah went back to the text and had students identify any signal words they noticed. She highlighted these words in green (see figure 2.3).

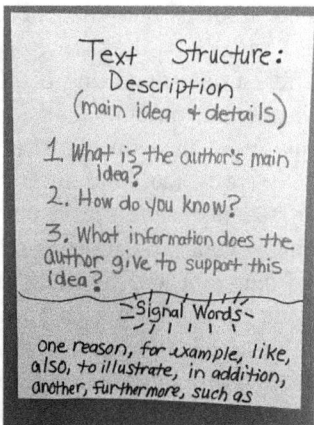
Figure 2.2. Text Structure Anchor Chart. *Source*: Mary Hoch.

Birds inhabit most of the earth. Each habitat poses unique challenges that birds must face. They need to adapt in order to survive. One of the most challenging places on earth for birds is the ocean. Some birds living near the ocean spend most of their lives in flight. As such, birds like the wandering albatross, have vast wingspans to make flight effortless. Others must adapt to freezing ocean water. Penguins have thick layers of waterproof feathers to help them survive freezing ocean conditions. Adaptations such as these have made it possible for birds to live almost anywhere.

Figure 2.3. Highlighted Signal Words. *Source*: Mary Hoch.

Since these words usually signal additional information about the author's idea, Sarah explained that they sometimes signal a sentence that contains supporting details. And, when this is the case, the main idea usually preceded. Main ideas are often, but certainly not always, presented at the precedes of a paragraph. Based on this premise, Sarah guided the students in using the signal words highlighted in green to identify the preceding main ideas. She highlighted the main ideas in pink (see figure 2.4).

Now they were ready to use the signal words and the main ideas to lead them to the supporting details. Sarah highlighted these in yellow (see figure 2.5).

You probably noticed that, when highlighting, Sarah only included keywords or phrases that were essential to the main idea or details. We agree with this approach and firmly believe that "less is more" when it comes to highlighting (more on this in chapter 4).

Returning to the anchor chart, Sarah helped students make the connections between what they just highlighted and the prompts. It was clear how the highlighted words and phrases provided sufficient textual evidence for responding to the prompts.

==Birds inhabit most of the earth==. Each habitat poses unique ==challenges== that birds must face. They need to ==adapt in order to survive==. One of the most challenging places on earth for birds is the ocean. Some birds living near the ocean spend most of their lives in flight. As such, birds like the wandering albatross, have vast wingspans to make flight effortless. Others must adapt to freezing ocean water. Penguins have thick layers of waterproof feathers to help them survive freezing ocean conditions. Adaptations such as these have made it possible for birds to live almost anywhere.

Figure 2.4.   Highlighted Main Ideas. *Source*: **Mary Hoch.**

==Birds inhabit most of the earth==. Each habitat poses unique ==challenges== that birds must face. They need to ==adapt in order to survive==. One of the most challenging places on earth for birds is the ocean. Some birds living near the ocean spend most of their lives in flight. As such, birds like the wandering albatross, have vast wingspans to make flight effortless. Others must adapt to freezing ocean water. Penguins have thick layers of waterproof feathers to help them survive freezing ocean conditions. Adaptations such as these have made it possible for birds to live almost anywhere.

Figure 2.5.   Highlighted Supporting Details. *Source*: **Mary Hoch.**

In subsequent mini-lessons, Sarah will gradually move toward independent practice by using this text structure to identify the main ideas and details with increasingly longer texts.

Once students seem to grasp the concept of this organization, Sarah will be ready to introduce the Structure Sort process.

CONNECTIONS

Based on the two classroom examples provided in this chapter, we hope to have made clear connections between teaching text structures and the Structure Sort process. Teaching text structures provides a foundation that is essential to the Structure Sort process. But just teaching text structures is not enough. Once the foundation is set, teachers are ready to begin adding Structure Sorts as the next layer in fostering comprehension of expository texts. Facilitating the interrelated processes of understanding text structures and the Structure Sort method is what we believe will empower readers to be successful in understanding expository texts.

Key Points

- Teaching text structures and the Structure Sort method are interrelated. Begin by laying the foundation with opportunities to learn about all five text structures.

- Use your knowledge of students and curriculum to determine which text structures you will focus on at specific times.
- Be sure to continuously read from a variety of text structures so students can compare the different structures and become familiar with identifying them in authentic reading situations.
- Ensure students are exposed to all five text structures at the beginning of the year and then continue to reinforce each structure throughout the year.
- Avoid using assessments that simply require students to "name the text structure." Rather, focus on what features of the text they notice, what text structure they think it is, and their reasons *why*.
- Incorporate explicit instruction and scaffolding for specific text structures as needed.

Chapter 3

Using Assessment to Drive the Process

> **CHAPTER FOCUS:** In this chapter we will focus on formatively assessing the component skills embedded in the Structure Sort method and how this information can be used to drive instruction.

> *Overall, the ancillary skills, such as reasoning, summarizing, and predicting, that go into being able to complete the sorts are what I find to be the most valuable. I am able to assess many reading skills within the sorts. For example, watching my students write predictions and summaries when the focus was on structure gives me lots of great information on what needs to be adjusted in my instruction.*
>
> —Owen, fourth-grade teacher

While considering how Structure Sorts could be used to drive instruction, the aforementioned quote from Owen, including how it embodies formative assessment practices that can lead to manifestations of understanding in several different ways, is essential. In other words, how can teachers measure cognitive processes that are not always visible? The assessment practices described in this chapter are ways of going beyond traditional comprehension assessment methods to do just that.

Vygoskian (1978) principles on gradually releasing responsibility guide teachers in determining how much support is needed and when students are ready for increased independence. As fierce proponents of constructivism, it is our firm believe that we need to learn about our students *formatively*, every step of the way.

Although we use the Structure Sort Graphic Organizer to help students think about expository texts, and while it produces a written end product that would be rather easy to evaluate, when assessing, we want to be clear about going beyond the students' ability to fill in the graphic organizer. In other words, the graphic organizer is intended to guide the students in their understanding of the text, rather than as a tool for evaluating whether their responses were "right" or "wrong." Therefore, when we consider how to assess understanding using the Structure Sort teaching method, we use five guiding factors:

1. *Continuous Assessment*—We know that teaching and learning need to be interactive processes. Formative assessment is one component of such processes. This involves gathering information that is produced during these interactions and using it to adapt teaching to meet students' needs (Black & Wiliam, 1998).

    First and foremost, formative assessment needs to take place during all three phases of reading: *before*, *during*, and *after*. It is not something that should be left for the end. Listening to students tell *how* they categorized words and their predictions and providing them with an opportunity to orally explain *why* they made such choices provides the teacher with a window into their thinking. Whether it be in partnerships, small groups, or whole group, social interactions through discussion provide teacher with opportunities for continuous assessment during all phases of reading.

2. *Authentic Understanding*—As already mentioned, it is our intention to guide teachers and students beyond the ability to fill in the blanks of the graphic organizer. Our intention is to assess their thinking for authentic understanding, which should be used to shape future instruction. Listening to how students worked their way through the Structure Sort helps teachers make determinations about their development and the level of authentic understanding gained.

3. *Stages of Development*—Learning is developmental and occurs in stages (Vygotsky, 1962, 1978; Wertsch, 1985). While we know our younger students may not yet have the mental capacity to organize information to understand it when beginning Structure Sorts, learning should be looked at individually and development described in terms of stages. For example, we like to use four stages to describe our students' development. Each stage describes their growth toward proficiency with understanding expository text: (1) attempting; (2) approaching; (3) meeting; and (4) exceeding.

4. *Discussion Points*—You have probably noticed that *listening* is a recurring practice that is embedded across formative assessment in the Structure

Sort teaching approach. For this important practice to occur, the approach to teaching must include points in the lesson where discussions can take place. Discussion is essential because it provides students with an opportunity to demonstrate learning and reveal important information about their background knowledge and allows them opportunities for active participation (Cazden, 2001). Through discussion, students have the opportunity to verbally justify their decisions in relation to strategy application.

We recommend two discussion points. The first should occur before reading—after the students have sorted their keywords and before they make their prediction. This will allow them to verbalize their thinking and get input from others. They can use this information to broaden their perspective and expand their thinking before making a prediction. The second discussion point should occur following the Read and Check and before they write their summary. This discussion point will help students confirm their thinking, solidify their decisions, and reason through their ideas. As the teacher listens to discussions, he or she should consider what their conversations reveal about their understanding.

5. *Writing*—Structure Sorts provide students with two opportunities for brief expository writing. These built-in writing opportunities serve as a tool for understanding. The end result is a synthesis of the student's thinking about the text. The power of writing as a tool for synthesizing understanding should not be underestimated.

When these five guiding factors are used simultaneously, assessment will naturally drive what we do next in terms of instruction.

ASSESSMENT IN THE *BEFORE-READING* PHASE

There are two steps that occur in the *before-reading* phase. The first is where students consider the words that the teacher has placed in the "keywords" box and decide how to sort them, in relation to the macrostructure of the text. To illustrate how assessment can occur during this phase, let's use an example from Owen's fourth-grade class.

Owen chose a cause and effect sort to help his students work their way through a Newsela article ("Scientist's Study," 2016). To teach his students how to use a cause and effect sort, Owen first chunked the text into manageable pieces, which was already nicely divided up by subheadings. To teach this structure, he used only the first chunk of text was comprised of five short paragraphs. He chose the following seven keywords to help his students identify the main causes and effects that the author would present in this portion of the article: *dangerous, burned, released, heat, traps, temperatures,* and *flooding*. Owen introduced the title of the article and read through the keywords with his class, and all students had a copy of the article. The students then individually sorted each of the seven words into the *cause* column or the *effect* column. The class was now ready for the first discussion point, which was Owen's first opportunity to assess.

Owen started with the first word, *dangerous*. He asked for a volunteer to share where they placed the word and why. Based on the student's oral response, Owen was able to ask follow-up questions to gently guide the student's thinking. This provided Owen with several insights about the student. First, it told him a little bit about the student's background knowledge on the topic. Second, and, importantly, it provided Owen with a good idea as to the student's ability to reason. That is, the column in which the student placed the word *dangerous* is of secondary importance to their ability to explain their logic for why they placed the word where they did. Owen invited a few more students to share word placements. Then all students were able to share their sorting decisions with a partner. After talking with their partner they could make any adjustments they felt were necessary. In the end, it was each student's decision how to sort the words.

Now they were ready for the second step of this phase, making a prediction. The goal of predicting in this approach is to hypothesize about the content based on the keywords and how we decided to sort them. We encourage students to use as many of the keywords as possible when writing a prediction. Once each student wrote a prediction, Owen gave them another opportunity to share their thinking with a partner and make any changes based on that conversation.

In the example of Jenny in figure 3.1, you can see that the student was not necessarily able to produce a rich prediction. In fact, she was only able to use two of the keywords in her prediction, *dangerous* and *flooding*, and she predicted both would be effects. It is also interesting to consider how she might hypothesize about flooding being caused by carbon dioxide. The point here is that as students work their way through the graphic organizer through reading and discussion points, thinking becomes deeper and responses richer. This information also provides us with some instructional implications. While Jenny was able to predict that carbon dioxide would likely be dangerous and cause flooding, we would want to push her a step further on future sorts. A good baby step would be to encourage Jenny and other students to add one more sentence telling how the words (or at least one word) in the *cause* column would be part of the cause. This requires her to extend her thinking. Or, if more scaffolding is indicated, the teacher could model how to add one more sentence to Jenny's prediction to hypothesize about the causes.

Handwritten Form Sample

Jenny

STRUCTURE SORT: Cause & Effect

TEXT TITLE: Scientists Study new uses for Carbon dioxide (intro)

KEY WORDS: dangerous, burned, released, heat, traps, temperatures, flooding

- **SORT**

CAUSE	+ or -	EFFECT	+ or -
temperatures	−	flooding	+
heat	+	dangerous	−
traps	−	burned	−
		released	+

- **PREDICT** I predict that the carbon dioxide will be really dangerous. And it may cause flooding.

Figure 3.1. Cause and Effect Structure Sort Sample. *Source:* Mary Hoch.

ASSESSMENT IN THE *DURING-READING* PHASE

The next step in the process is for students to read the chunk of text and check how they sorted their keywords when they encounter them in text. While this seems like a simple enough step, checking how they sorted their words while reading actually requires a great deal of cognitive energy. First, the student must be able to construct meaning at the sentence level. In addition, the students must be able to synthesize meaning at a broader level—in relation to the paragraph, as well as the entire chunk of text. And, finally, the student must be able to reason about whether or not their sorting decision was correct, and why or why not, which leads to a deeper understanding of a particular keyword in relation to the structure of the text. Let's consider this using the previously mentioned example of Jenny. The first paragraph of the article reads:

> Carbon dioxide is a gas. It can be dangerous. Every year billions of tons end up in our air. This causes big problems for the Earth.

Jenny initially placed the word *dangerous* in the effect column, which implied that dangerous conditions might be an effect of carbon dioxide. While Jenny's action is certainly reasonable, upon reading the article Jenny marked a minus next to this word because she was able to piece together the idea that carbon dioxide was dangerous because it leads to various problems for the planet. This required an understanding of the keyword, her ability to synthesize meaning in this context, and being able to reason and make a determination about her decision.

Now students are ready for the second discussion point. We realize not all students, especially our younger ones, are able to meet the cognitive demands in the way that Jenny did. After the Read and Check, students need a second opportunity to talk with peers to once again be able to confirm, reason, and extend their thinking about whether or not their sorting decisions were correct and why or why not. It is these conversations that reveal the students' level of *authentic understanding*, what additional scaffolding might be necessary, and what the next steps need to be in terms of the teacher's instruction.

ASSESSMENT IN THE *AFTER-READING* PHASE

After reading, checking their sorting decisions, and discussion with peers, the final step in the process is to summarize after reading. We know, as teachers, the importance of being able to summarize in a way that is succinct and meaningful. We also know this is a very difficult skill for many students, especially those who struggle. Throughout this approach the keywords have been used to guide students' thinking about the text. The *after reading* summary is where we can assess each student's evolution of thinking. The goal here is, again, to use as many keywords as possible to demonstrate understanding of the key ideas that the author has conveyed. It is important here to consider each student's growth over time. So, as students practice the Structure Sort strategy, we want to assess the richness of their summary as well as their proficiency to produce a succinct summary.

There are two measures of growth we like to consider. The first is students' ability to accurately express the main ideas of the text using more keywords than they included in their prediction. To illustrate, take a look at Jenny's summary in figure 3.2. While Jenny's summary was only three sentences, she doubled the amount of keywords when comparing her summary to her prediction. In addition, we can see that each keyword was used correctly and, most importantly, her summary is accurate and clearly identifies the author's main ideas. This is quite an accomplishment! We would consider Jenny's performance on this Structure Sort to be *meeting* the level of proficiency we

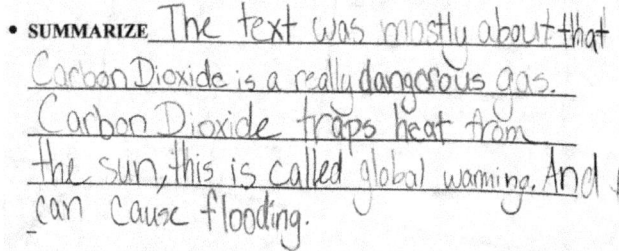

Figure 3.2. Cause and Effect Structure Sort Sample Summary. *Source*: Mary Hoch.

would expect for this sort, at this particular point in time, and in relation to past performance.

The second measure of growth we consider is if the student was able to accurately express the main ideas of the text using more keywords than they did on their last summary. While, by no means, do we wish to quantify student responses on the graphic organizer, this is just a suggestion for helping students strive for rich summaries over time. This way of considering assessment also points to the importance of choosing keywords that are high utility and essential to meaning.

A STEP FURTHER

While we can't stress enough the importance of including two discussion points to assess students' understanding and help them extend their thinking, Owen shared a way in which he is able to quickly see a snapshot of student learning, digitally, all in one place. Owen uses Padlet (https://padlet.com) as a way of having students share their work with each other, while allowing him to formatively assess and consider each student's stage of development. Padlet is an app that creates an online "bulletin board" where one can interactively display and share information. Owen asked his students to share their Structure Sort summary on a Padlet he created. This is an easy way to ramp up engagement while also providing another opportunity for students to learn from each other. A sample Padlet from the same unit discussed earlier in this chapter can be viewed in figure 3.3.

In this chapter we discussed our view of assessment and how to formatively assess in a way that focuses on student growth. We described five guiding factors that lead the way through the Structure Sort teaching approach. We then described what formative assessment looks like during all the three phases of reading. In the chapters ahead, implementation of each type of Structure Sort will be described to help you get started.

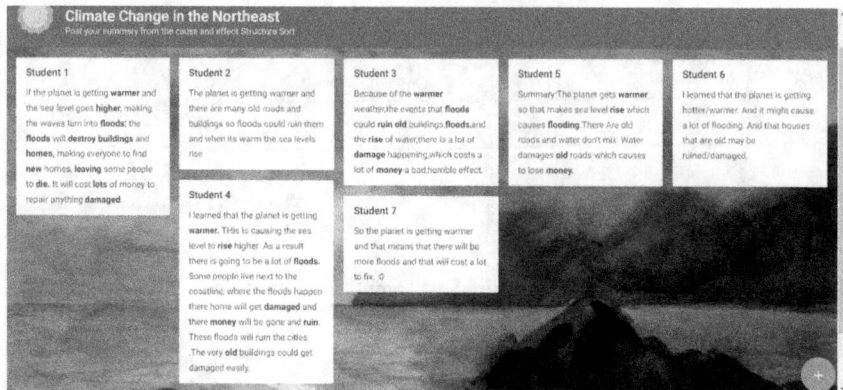

Figure 3.3.   Padlet Sample. *Source*: Mary Hoch.

Key Points

- There are many opportunities to assess throughout the Structure Sort process. Use these opportunities to measure students' cognitive processes that might otherwise not be visible.
- Rely on formative practices to assess during all three phases of reading. This is what drives your next instructional moves.
- Assess authentic understanding by listening to students as they share their thinking rather than assessing "right" or "wrong" responses on the graphic organizer.
- When assessing, consider growth toward proficiency with understanding expository text.
- Discussion points are essential to the Structure Sort process. Use them as opportunities for students to demonstrate new learning.
- Use writing as a tool for students to synthesize their understanding of the text.

Chapter 4

Description

> **CHAPTER FOCUS: In this chapter we will focus on how a teacher prepares for implementation of the Structure Sort in their classroom.**

A few weeks before a second-grade classroom was about to take "the big test," all twenty-two students were clutching a different colored highlighter in each hand, bent over a piece of text, and highlighting every single line of text.

"What are they working on?" Jana asked their teacher.

"Main idea and detail," she proudly replied. "Every word that is part of the main idea is yellow, and every word that is part of the detail is green."

Jana stared at twenty-two pieces of paper bleeding green and yellow. In some cases, the papers were so saturated with color that they were ripping apart.

Somehow (most likely due to the testing culture of our school systems) the concept of a main idea and a detail became such a focus in classrooms that in many cases, students believed every single word of a text had to be categorized as part of the main idea or a detail. Highlighting every word in a text not only is time consuming and a waste of those expensive highlighters but also completely misses the purpose of highlighting—bringing into view the most essential point of the text.

When a student reads a descriptive text, we want them to be able to identify the most important idea of the description, as well as what details support that idea. However, not every single word needs to be categorized as one or the other. The example of Sarah in chapter 2, describes a "less is more" approach when it comes to highlighting, which we believe to be highly effective.

A descriptive text gives information about a person, place, thing, or idea. Authors use description to structure text in a way that provides the reader with a key idea, and supporting details that tell about the idea. Descriptions usually contain definitions and examples, which are some of the identifying features of this structure. When we give our students a piece of descriptive text, we want them to be able to understand the main idea of the text and use the important details as evidence to support these ideas. This is not an easy task. A descriptive Structure Sort works as a scaffold to assist students in wading through the facts, details, descriptions, and vocabulary to accomplish the task of comprehension. In this chapter, we will walk you through the teacher's journey to find a descriptive text, select the keywords, and finally put the Structure Sort into action. We begin by presenting a sample piece of text similar to text you may find in magazines, textbooks, or online resources for students.

THE EMOJI LANGUAGE

If someone asked you how your day was, you might say "good" or "great." But, if you use a phone or tablet, the answer would probably be [☺] or [👍]. Emoji has quickly become the language of choice for people across the globe. Every year, Apple © introduces us to hundreds of new emojis. Some of the newest emojis include a bagel, cupcake, and firecracker. Emoji is a language that helps us share our feelings and ideas. But where did this new language come from?

Emojis were invented in Japan in 1999. At first, there were 176 emojis including a heart, sun, telephone, and snowman. The emoji language is like the way ancient Egyptians communicated many years ago. They used symbols called hieroglyphs to communicate. For example, hieroglyphs included images of animals, things, and people. Later, they stood for ideas and words, just like emojis do today. What emoji do you hope Apple introduces next?

Imagine now you are a second-grade teacher planning a short research project with your students on emojis. You have selected the above text for your students as you begin your research project. Using a Structure Sort will give your students a launching pad to wade through the research and pull out the important details needed to begin learning about the beloved emoji.

PREPARING FOR A DESCRIPTION STRUCTURE SORT

What follows is a model of the thinking processes that we imagine a teacher taking as they begin the Structure Sort process.

Step One: **Determine the structure of the expository text selection**

Based on title alone, I think this is a chronological text because it says it is about the emoji language, so I am assuming it may be a chronological history of the emoji language. However, as I read through the paragraph, I realize it not only gives a bit of history of the emoji, but it also describes what an emoji is and shares the new emojis being released. When I look at the Structure Sorts, I am a little torn between Sequence and Description. I know that authors often use more than one structure in a text, so I need to consider the overall macrostructure as well as look at the purpose before I decide.

Step Two: **Identify the purpose for reading**

I want my students to learn what an emoji is and how it entered our mainstream society. When thinking about my purpose, I feel this paragraph fits better as a descriptive text because I want my students focused on the main idea of this text as well as a few important supporting details. In addition, the overall macrostructure of the text seems to be a description of emojis, so I will stick with Description.

Step Three: **Select six to nine keywords from the text directly related to the purpose and key ideas or concepts**

Before selecting the keywords, I first decided to write my own main idea summary sentences so that I could choose the keywords from my own summary. So, when I think about what is important for my students to know about emojis, the sentence I come up with is, "Emojis are images that communicate feelings." I also want my students to know, "Images have been used to communicate for many years." From these sentences, the key words from the text that come to mind are: emojis, communicate, feelings, and image. When I review the whole text again, the word hieroglyphs stands out as a tier 3 word, and the words invented and symbols stand out as tier 2 words. This leaves me with the following words: emoji, communicate, feelings, image, hieroglyphs, invented, and symbol.

The teacher preparation phase is now complete and the Structure Sort is ready to be introduced to the second-grade students.

BEFORE READING

Sort

Students now have a Structure Sort in front of them (see figure 4.1). It is recommended that the teacher read the title and each of the keywords aloud to students before they begin to sort. Students will now place each of the

Description

TEXT TITLE: The Emoji Language

KEY WORDS: **emoji, feelings, hieroglyphs, symbols, invented, images, communicate**

- SORT

MAIN IDEA	+ or -	DETAIL	+ or -

- PREDICT _____

  _____

  _____

  _____

- READ & CHECK (+ or -)

- SUMMARIZE _____

  _____

  _____

  _____

Figure 4.1. Description Structure Sort Sample. *Source:* Jana McNally.

keywords in the category where they predict they will belong. For example, a student may place the keywords as follows:

Main idea	Detail
Emoji	Invented
Communicate	Hieroglyphs
Symbol	Feelings
	Image

After the students have placed their words, it is important to allow time for discussion. This can be done as a whole group or with a partner. A driving force behind this strategy is that students are able to tell not only *how* they sorted keywords but also *why* they sorted the way they did. As a pre-reading strategy, there really is no right or wrong way to sort the words, as long as the students can orally justify their decisions. For example, many of the words listed earlier could be explained as being a main idea or a detail depending on the student's prior knowledge. A student may place *communicate* in the detail column because it is a specific thing that emojis could be used for. Or, *hieroglyphs* might be justified as a main idea because it's a word that the author will probably define. The point here is to take time to allow students to work through their thinking and reason through their decisions in a way that promotes high-level understanding. The ability to justify and reason is what leads to empowerment in our readers.

Predict

After this discussion, the students are prompted to write a prediction of what they think the article will be about based on the keywords. The way they have sorted the words will help them in constructing what they think will be a text-based prediction. Students should be encouraged to use as many keywords as possible in their prediction. For example, using these keywords, a student may write the following prediction: "I predict the emoji was invented to show feelings."

DURING READING

Read and Check

Students now have the opportunity to read the text and check their placement of the keywords. As they read and encounter the keywords in text, they should decide if they agree with where they placed the word. If they feel their word is in the correct category, they would place a plus (+) next to the word. If they feel they put a word in the wrong category, they would place a minus (−) next to the word. So, when looking at the earlier example, a student's Read and Check may look like the following:

Main idea	Detail
Emoji +	Invented +
Communicate +	Hieroglyphs +
Symbol −	Feelings −
	Image −

As stated previously, the key here is not for students to have correctly sorted the words the first time around. Rather, the Read and Check step keeps students engaged in the text and helps them monitor their comprehension. Completion of the Read and Check serves as another great discussion point

STRUCTURE SORT: Description

TEXT TITLE: **The Emoji Language**

KEY WORDS: **emoji, communicate, feelings, image, hieroglyphs, invented, and symbol**

- SORT

MAIN IDEA	+ or -	DETAIL	+ or -
emoji	+	invented	+
communicate	+	hieroglyphs	+
symbol	−	feelings	−
		image	−

- PREDICT **The emoji was invented to show feelings.**

- READ & CHECK (+ or -)
- SUMMARIZE **Emojis are symbols that were invented to show feelings.**

Figure 4.2. Description Structure Sort Student Sample. *Source*: Jana McNally.

for the group to meet as a whole, or in partners, to flesh out their thinking about their second sort of keywords. Time to discuss and reason at this point will empower students to be able to construct a summary in the final step.

AFTER READING

Summarize

During this final step, students will write a summary of the text using the keywords for support. For example, the student may write, "Emojis are symbols. They were invented to show feelings." Another student may write something like, "Emojis are images and my favorite emoji is the poop emoji." (Second graders love to talk about poop!) This summary gives students an opportunity to synthesize their understanding of the text with the support of the keywords. It also provides an opportunity for each student to share their own unique synthesis with one another since each student's background knowledge gives them their own own-of-a-kind reading experience. Sharing their summaries with one another promotes classroom discourse and further engages students with the expository text. A completed Structure Sort can be seen in figure 4.2.

Key Points

- Highlighting an entire page of text is not productive. A Structure Sort for descriptive text will keep the focus narrow and succinct.
- When determining text structure, it is important to look at the overall macrostructure, rather than considering microstructures that may exist at the paragraph level. The emoji example had chronological components to it, but the overall purpose fit with the descriptive text structure.
- Do not get caught up in putting words into the "correct" category of main idea or detail. The point is to take time to allow students to work through and discuss their thinking to promote high-level understanding of the text.

Chapter 5

Problem and Solution

> **CHAPTER FOCUS: In this chapter we will focus on the Structure Sort as a read-aloud as well as strategies for working with emergent readers.**

Preschool, kindergarten, and elementary classrooms are dominated by genres such as fairy tales, folk tales, fantasy, tall tales, science fiction, and realistic fiction. Each of these fictional genres generally follows the traditional plot structure which includes an introduction (problem or conflict is introduced), rising action (action leading to the climax), climax (high point of interest/turning point in story), falling action (problem begins to resolve), and resolution (problem is solved/story is concluded). Most elementary classrooms use a story map to teach plot and support comprehension of these fictional stories. Although there are hundreds of variations of story maps, almost every story map includes a space for characters, setting, problem, and solution. As a result, problem-solution is often the text structure students are most familiar with.

Because students are used to problem-solution in a fictional story, this provides an excellent transition into helping them identify the problem-solution structure in an expository text. It is important that teachers discuss the explicit differences between problem-solution in fiction and problem-solution in nonfiction. For example, the characters and setting in a fictional story are often magical characters in made-up places. The characters and setting in expository text are real people in real settings. In addition, the rising action, climax, and falling action of a fictional story usually include multiple action scenes. In an expository text it may instead be several potential solutions and why they did or did not work. In contrast to fictional stories, expository problem-solution text will usually include explicit keywords such as *problem* and *solution* or *question* and *answer*. Both fiction and nonfiction problem-solution text structures usually introduce the problem early on and resolve the text with a solution or potential solution.

As we explore the problem-solution text structure, we will be joining our youngest readers (age five) as they work with Jana to explore one of their favorite topics: Legos!

TOO MANY LEGOS

Have you ever felt the pain of a plastic Lego on the bottom of your bare foot? Chances are, you or someone in your household has. Approximately 100 million children around the world played with Legos in 2015. This holiday season, millions of children are asking for the newest Lego sets to add to their growing collection. The only problem: what to do with the thousands of Lego pieces laying around your house once you have finished building the set. These loose Legos cause foot pain, clutter, and frustration all around.

One solution is to leave the completed set on display without taking the pieces apart. There is even a new Lego glue to help keep the set together. This ensures the loose Lego pieces stay away from the floor and a house stays clutter-free. However, if the creation is just collecting dust on a shelf, children lose the chance for creative play.

Other children will build their set and then immediately destroy it and place it in a bag with the instructions. This allows them to take it out and rebuild it on a future date using the instructions to guide them once again.

Another option is to build your Lego set, take it apart, and then put it back together in your own new way. Some children have bins with tens of thousands of Lego pieces from multiple sets to make their own creations through free building. This method of building, rebuilding, designing, and visualizing sparks imagination and keeps the loose Legos off the floor: a win for everyone.

PREPARING FOR A PROBLEM-SOLUTION STRUCTURE SORT

The group of kindergarteners in this chapter are all considered emergent readers and would therefore not be able to read this text independently. However, we felt choosing a topic that was highly engaging for them (Legos) and allowing the teacher to read the text out loud to the students would place this normally higher-level text at their comprehension level. We also wanted to show how a Structure Sort can be used with a group of emergent readers using several modifications to make it a powerful strategy for our earliest readers.

Step One: Determine the structure of the expository text selection

The title "Too Many Legos" immediately jumps out as a problem that can be easily identified by this group of five-year-olds who all have extensive Lego collections. It is important to use the background knowledge of students when selecting a text, especially when they are first introduced to this strategy. Background knowledge will boost their comprehension and help them connect and engage with the text.

Throughout the short article, there are several strong phrases that clearly indicate a problem-solution text structure: "the only problem," "one solution," and "another option." These phrases guide readers' understanding of the text and make this article one of the more easily identifiable text structures.

Step Two: Identify the purpose for reading

Because we had an emergent group of readers, we wanted a text that would present a clear macrostructure for problem-solution. The purpose was for students to become familiar with a problem-solution text structure and to show comprehension of expository text. We felt the problem (*the only problem: what to do with the thousands of Lego pieces laying around your house once you have finished building the set*) was explicitly stated for the students which would aid them as they worked out the differences between problem and solution.

Step Three: Select six to nine keywords from the text directly related to the purpose and key ideas or concepts

Because this text was done with emergent five-year-old readers, only six words were selected: pain, clutter, display, creation, frustration, and rebuild. Each of these words were selected because they were clearly part of the problem and solution. In addition, these terms were all tier 2 words that, with some assistance, the students could connect with and add to their growing vocabularies.

BEFORE READING

Before reading the text, Jana asked, "What is a problem?" Some of their answers included "something bad," "something you need to solve," or "I don't like problems." They were then asked to think of an example of a problem together. They agreed on the problem, "When we don't have enough popsicles for everyone but you still want to eat them." Students were then asked to each think of a way to solve the problem. Some of their ideas included, "buying more popsicles" and "sharing popsicles." This led to a discussion of problem-solution. Before reading the text, it is important that students have ample time to discuss the text structure. This is especially true when the text structure is first introduced. As time goes on and students are fully comfortable and familiar with the text structure, this is a step that can be dramatically shortened or even skipped.

Sort

For this small group of kindergarteners, the keywords were read out loud to them one at a time. After reading each word, the group discussed what the word meant, and then decided as a group where the word should go. Jana then wrote the word on a Structure Sort anchor chart (see figure 5.1) for the students. Below is a snapshot of the discussion of the first word, "clutter."

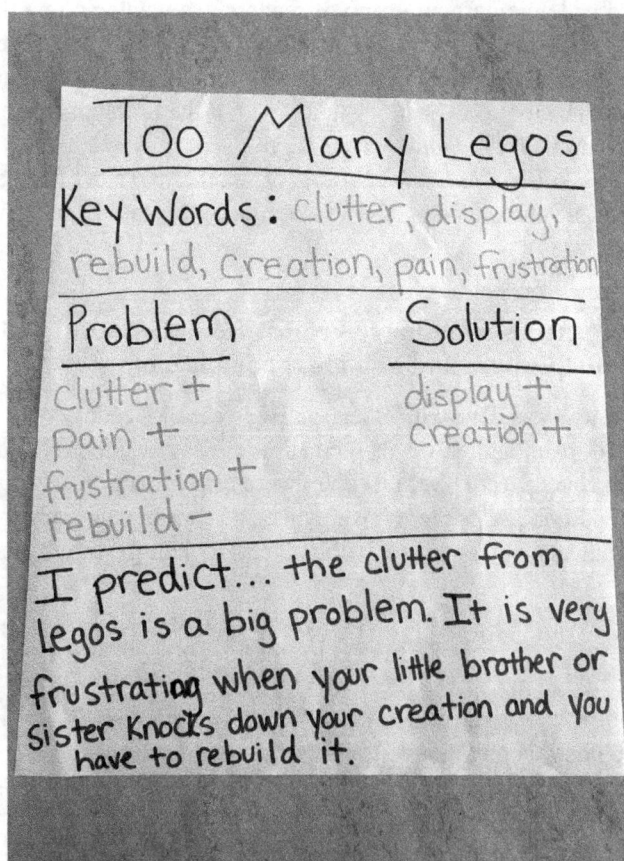

Figure 5.1. Problem and Solution Structure Sort Anchor Chart. *Source*: Jana McNally.

Jana: Our first word is *clutter*. What do you think *clutter* means?

Thomas: My mom hates clutter!

Will: When there is clutter you have to clean up.

Ruby: I think Santa comes down the chimney with a clutter.

Thomas: No! That's a clatter!

As a group, Jana guided students to define clutter as "a mess." Students were then asked if clutter sounded like it would be part of the problem or the solution.

Ruby: It sounds like a problem.

Oliver: Definitely a problem.

Thomas: My mom says clutter is a big problem in my room.

The discussion continued in a similar manner for each of the words. The students sorted the words as follows:

Problem	Solution
Clutter	Display
Pain	Creation
Frustration	
Rebuild	

Predict

Jana then modeled how to use the words to write a prediction. She used a "think-aloud" model so students could explicitly hear her thinking process as she used the words to write a prediction.

> *Hmmm.... I am going to use the title to help me predict. The title is "Too Many Legos" so it sounds like that is a big problem. I am thinking the problem might be clutter from all the Legos. What do you think the problem could be? How do the words pain, frustration, and rebuild add to the problem? And what could some of the solutions to the problem be?*

The students and Jana discussed ideas about the problem and solution, and as a group, they developed the following prediction: "The clutter from Legos is a big problem. It is very frustrating when your little brother or sister knocks down your creation and you have to rebuild it." This prediction showed students had an understanding of several keywords, as well as a strong connection to the potential frustrations of Legos. Students were now ready to "read" the article.

DURING READING

As mentioned earlier, the students in this group are emergent readers who are unable to independently read text. Therefore, this text was used as a read-aloud. Jana chose to read the text twice. During the first read, she allowed students to stop and discuss the problems and solutions. The purpose here was a focus on the text structure and comprehension. During the second read, she stopped after each keyword so that students could perform the "read and check." Below is a snapshot of their discussion of the word *rebuild*.

> *Jana:* "This allows them to take it out and *rebuild* it on a future date using the instructions to guide them once again." Did anyone hear one of our keywords there?
>
> *Will:* Rebuild!
>
> *Jana:* Great. So what do you think? Is rebuild part of the problem or the solution?
>
> *Thomas:* Keep it in problem!
>
> *Jana:* Why?
>
> *Thomas:* Because we got all of them right so far.
>
> *Jana:* What does everyone else think?
>
> *Oliver:* I think it's a solution.
>
> *Will:* Me too.
>
> *Ruby:* Me too.
>
> *Jana:* Why do you think that?
>
> *Will:* Because when you rebuild it you are making it better so you fixed the problem.
>
> *Thomas:* Yea it's a solution!

See the anchor chart in figure 5.1 for the completed read and check.

Problem	Solution
Clutter +	Creation +
Pain +	Display +
Frustration +	
Rebuild −	

AFTER READING

At the end of the Structure Sort, Jana modeled writing a summary with the kindergarten students. She suggested to the students, "Let's write about what this article was about. First we will write a sentence about the problem, and then we will write a sentence about the solution." She also encouraged students to use the keywords. To scaffold their writing process, Jana provided students with the following sentence starters to aid in their sentence construction:

Too many Legos can be a problem because _____.
Some solutions include _____.

As students shared ideas, Jana wrote their sentences on anchor chart paper. When all the ideas had been added, the students selected the two sentences that they felt best summarized the article (see figure 5.2).

> *Too many Legos can be a problem because they make clutter in the house and pain when you step on them. Some solutions include putting your Legos away in a bin and rebuilding them to make new creations.*

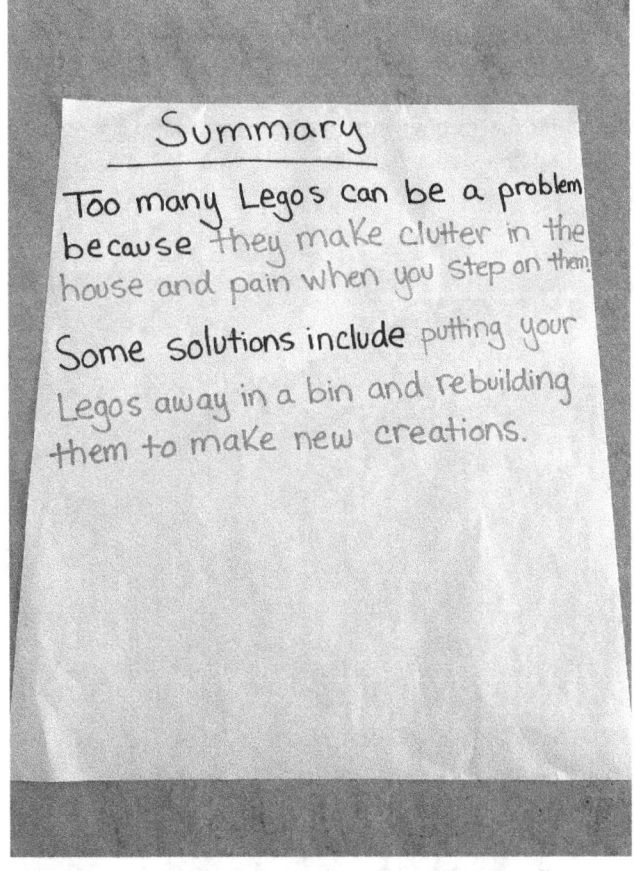

Figure 5.2. Shared Summary Writing Sample. *Source*: Jana McNally.

Their final summary demonstrated both comprehension of the text and understanding of the text structure. This entire lesson was done as a group with Jana providing extensive scaffolding and modeling. While this lesson has been adapted to meet the needs of emergent learners, subsequent chapters demonstrate implementation geared more toward critical thinking and gained independence.

Key Points

- Before beginning a sort, it is important that students have ample time to discuss the text structure. As students become familiar with the various structures, this is a step that can be shortened or even skipped.
- Use students' familiarity with the problem-solution text structure of fiction to your advantage. Be sure to discuss the explicit differences between problem-solution in fiction compared to nonfiction.
- Your emergent readers can and should participate in Structure Sorts. Accommodations for these early readers can include extensive teacher modeling, teacher read-aloud of the text, shared writing, and/or sentence starters.
- Give students time to discuss the keywords and share their personal connections to each word.
- Select a text topic that your emergent readers are familiar with so they can use their background knowledge to make connections to aid their comprehension.

Chapter 6

Sequence

CHAPTER FOCUS: In this chapter we will focus on helping students use keywords to make strong predictions Before Reading and monitor comprehension During Reading.

"How was your day?"

This question is asked by millions of parents to their children after school, when the parents get home from work, at the dinner table, in the car, or before bed. What follows often depends on the age of the child. For example, a five-year-old may ramble through an exact timeline of every mundane detail of their day including what cereal they ate, how many bathroom breaks they took at school, and which television shows they watched. A teenager instead may utter the classic "fine" with no further details.

To begin this chapter, let's focus on the five-year-old for a moment. When young children retell their days, they usually do so sequentially, reliving each moment starting with breakfast and continuing through the day until they reach the moment where you asked them how their day was. As children get older, they learn to synthesize and summarize the information to share only the highlights and important details. And then at some point they decide to share nothing, but that's an entirely different book.

Young children often view the world sequentially, which is why they thrive on routines. They know that after breakfast comes teeth brushing. After teeth brushing comes hair. After hair comes getting their shoes on for school. And so on throughout the day. These routines are encouraged as young as birth to establish healthy sleep patterns. "First bath, then diaper, then pajamas, then bottle, then bed." Although, coming from two mothers whose combined five infants never slept, this advice is certainly subject to debate. Either way, children have a natural and innate sense of sequence from a very early age.

As a result, sequential (also called chronological) text structures can be one of the more reader-friendly text structures for young students to identify. It often includes signal words such as *first*, *next*, *then*, and *finally*. Some common forms of nonfiction sequential texts include how-tos, recipes, instruction manuals, news reports, and historical timelines.

Sequence is also the format used in teaching writing at an early age. Children as young as preschool are given graphic organizers with boxes for the beginning, middle, and end, or *first*, *next*, and *last*. They are encouraged to draw and "write" the beginning, middle, and end whether they retell a story or tell about their weekend. This makes the sequential text structure an important text structure to introduce to students at an early age as they continue to build their schema for sequential text writing models.

One way to integrate sequential text structures is through a classroom's current events curriculum. Many classrooms designate time during social studies or literacy blocks to share current events articles about their local community, state, country, or world. Many of these articles are written in the sequential text structure, which offers an excellent opportunity to use a Structure Sort to comprehend and discuss the article chosen.

In this chapter, we follow Mary's implementation in Kayla Gray's third-grade classroom, where they explored a local current events article using the Structure Sort as their guide.

TREE TOWN PRESCHOOL GIVES THANKS

Students in Mrs. Jones four-year-old preschool class spent the month of November discussing things they were thankful for and looking for ways to give back to their local community. They began the month brainstorming ideas for how to show their thanks for their local community. Several of their initial ideas included a food drive, cleaning up garbage in the neighboring park, sending letters of thanks to local community members, and collecting books for a school in need. After listening to the ideas, students voted on holding a classroom food drive with their favorite nonperishable foods.

To begin, students decorated giant cardboard boxes to look like turkeys including colorful feathers and snoods. Next, students created a list of their favorite nonperishable food items. These included macaroni and cheese, cans of alphabet letters with red sauce, boxes of cereal, and even condiments like ketchup and mustard. Each student then took their favorite food list home to their families to use as a grocery list. Students shopped with their families and then brought in their favorite food items throughout the month.

"My favorite part was feeding the cardboard turkey with boxes of pasta," said student Theo Wilkens.

In addition to collecting the food items, students enjoyed categorizing and counting their growing collection each day. The final step involved lining up each food item down the long hallway outside their classroom before making the final count of 457 items collected. These items were donated to the South County Food Pantry.

"It's wonderful to see students as young as four engaged in giving back to our community," said South County Food Pantry director Kim Nevens. "These students are true models for the joy that comes from giving."

PREPARING FOR A SEQUENCE STRUCTURE SORT

Step One: Determine the structure of the expository text selection

Every week, Kayla's third-grade class reads an article from the local community newspaper. Kayla has found this to be an excellent source for accessible, relatable, and engaging informational texts for her students. This set the stage for Mary to utilize such a selection to further students' comprehension through the integrated strategies of the Structure Sort method. When reviewing this article, many sequential keywords and phrases jumped out right away: *began, initial, to begin, next, in addition,* and *the final step*. In looking at the article as a whole, Mary determined that it was a summary of the steps preschool students took to complete a successful food drive. Each of these factors made it easily identifiable as sequential text structure.

Step Two: Identify the purpose for reading

Beyond using the sequential nature of the article to build understanding, Kayla noted some general concerns with her students' predictions, which, oftentimes, seemed unfocused and disconnected from text. Thus, Mary decided this would be an excellent focus for this text. The goal was for students to be able to use prediction as a way to consider the outcome of the events they would read about. She would guide them in forming strong predictions based on keywords and using both to monitor their understanding while reading, so that a sequential summary could result.

Step Three: Select six to nine keywords from the text directly related to the purpose and key ideas or concepts.

To select the keywords, Mary decided to first jot down the steps the students in the article took to complete a successful food drive. She came up with

1. Brainstorm ideas
2. Vote on an idea

3. Nonperishable food drive selected
4. Decorate food collection box as a turkey
5. Students create list of food items
6. Students shop for and collect food items in classroom
7. Students categorized food items
8. Students donated food items

This list helped her to select the keywords that were part of each step and that were necessary to comprehend the steps. Her list was as follows:

Brainstorm, ideas, non-perishable, decorate, collect, categorize, donate

Because these words were selected in a sequential order, Mary made sure to mix them up before including them on the Structure Sort graphic organizer.

BEFORE READING

Mary started the lesson with the whole class gathered in front of her on the carpet. Since predicting would be a focus, she wanted to be sure to activate their background knowledge.

> *So, boys and girls, today we are going to learn about how a group of kids created a project that helped their community. Think for a minute, can any of you share events that take place in the community you live in?*

Students shared examples such as an upcoming local 5K run called a "Turkey Trot" that a sibling would be running in; visiting a haunted house during a Fall Festival; and Open House at school, where parents recently got to visit classrooms. Mary also wanted to help them make the connection between what they would read and previously read articles from the local community newspaper.

> *I know that Miss Gray shares interesting articles with you each week on current events. Can anyone recall something interesting you read about recently?*

Since this was a regular occurrence in Kayla's class, students eagerly shared articles in which they learned about a Dr. Seuss celebration, a local library's book club, and the reopening of a community park.

Since substantial connections were made, Mary was now ready to introduce the new article and the Structure Sort method. She used a document camera to display only the article's title.

> *This week, Miss Gray and I wanted to share a new article with you about a community project. But before you read it, we're going to ask you to make some predictions about this event. To do this, I'm even going to give you some word clues to help you predict. But first, let's look at the title: Tree Town Preschool Gives Thanks. What could this article be about?*

Interestingly, because of the time of year, students were able to connect to the idea that "giving thanks" had something to do with Thanksgiving. However, that was as far as they got, and overall, no further connections could be made based on the title alone. This exemplifies how using keywords to predict in the Structure Sort method significantly improves students' ability to predict a possible, viable outcome.

Next, Mary used chart paper to reveal the seven keywords or "clues": *decorate, collect, ideas, donate, brainstorm, nonperishable,* and *categorize.*

> *Are you ready for your word clues? Let's read through them together and consider what they might mean. Think about which words you know and which words you aren't sure of. Use the words you know to rethink your prediction. Tree Town Preschool Gives Thanks. Decorate, collect, ideas, donate, brainstorm, nonperishable, categorize. Turn and talk to your neighbor about your prediction for this event. Use all the words you know as clues.*

Upon reconvening, students were mostly able to use words like *ideas, decorate, collect,* and *donate* to make predictions about the event. This helped move student thinking from title-only predictions, such as "I think the preschool kids will be thankful because it's Thanksgiving," to keyword-based predictions, such as, "The preschoolers might show they are thankful by decorating or donating things" and "The event might be where they come up with ideas to collect stuff and donate it." While the keyword-based predictions are not perfect, they are significantly more text-related and meaningful.

While no students were able to use the word *nonperishable* in their prediction, Mary decided not to predefine the word so that students could try to use context to determine its meaning. It would also provide an opportunity to self-monitor. She would revisit word meaning after completing the *after reading* task.

Now Mary was ready to help the students use the sequential organization of the text to further strengthen their predictions.

> *I'm going to give you one more clue to help you think some more about this event before we read about it. In this article, the author used sequence to organize the big ideas. So, if we take another look at our seven keywords, which do you think occurred first?*

Mary used the chart paper to order the words based on the students' suggestions. The students collectively agreed that *brainstorm* would be first and *ideas* would be second. There were discrepancies among the group about the remaining words, but the point is it got the students thinking deeply about the order of the words in finalizing their predictions. They independently decided upon the order and listed the words on their graphic organizer.

They were now ready to construct a written prediction based on the three essential components of this article: (1) the title; (2) the keywords; and (3) the anticipated sequence of the events.

DURING READING

For this lesson, students would be reading the article independently and then conferring with a partner on the order of events. In addition, we wanted students to monitor their understanding while reading.

> *As you Read and Check and decide whether or not your placement of each word was accurate, I'd also like you to work on monitoring for understanding. So, use each keyword as a stopping point to think about whether or not you understood the event that occurred. Let's start together.*

Mary read the first two sentences of the article aloud, and then modeled her thinking about the two keywords contained in the second sentence.

> *Here's what I'm thinking: I just read two keywords: brainstorm and ideas. I was correct in placing these words in the left-hand column because they were part of the first event in the article. So I will place a + in each of the boxes. But now I want to stop and make sure I understand what the author just told me. The author said that a preschool class wanted to help their community so they brainstormed ideas of how they could give back. Now I'm ready to read on. But what could I have done if I wasn't able to paraphrase in this way?*

Students suggested ideas such as rereading, checking with a partner, and annotating with a "?" as options in response to Mary's questions, all of which were excellent strategies to support self-monitoring.

AFTER READING

When students were done with the Read and Check portion, they met with a partner to discuss the order of events in the article as well as their understanding of what took place. Next, the whole group reconvened on the carpet. Students shared that they were confident in their understanding of the events they read about. To guide them in their sequential summary, Mary redirected them to the chart paper. She led them in numbering the keywords in the order they appeared in the article (see figure 6.1). But she also wanted to be sure they were able to extract meaning by asking if there were any words the students still did not

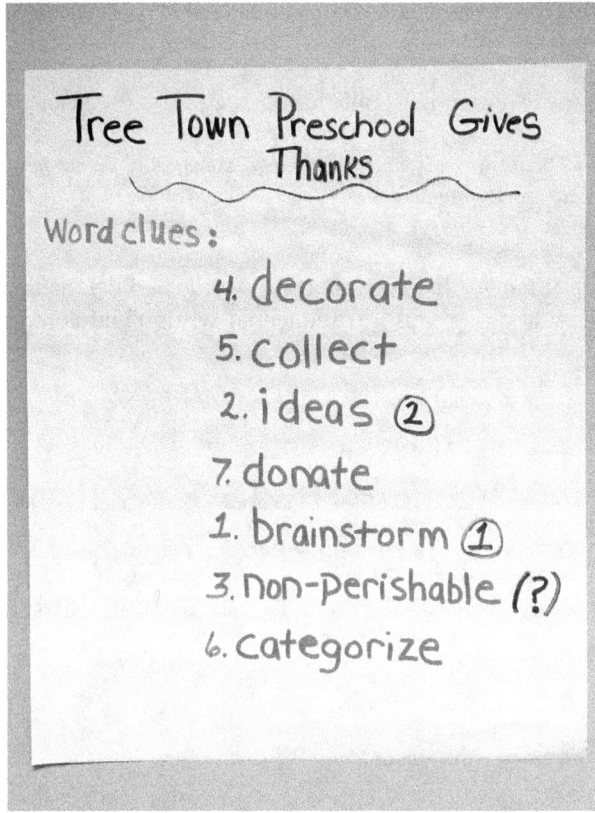

Figure 6.1. Keyword Anchor Chart for Sequence. *Source:* Mary Hoch.

understand or if they placed any question marks in the margins, as suggested earlier. *Nonperishable* was the one word that students were still unsure of.

Mary pointed out the context of this word.

The author tells us the kids are collecting the food items in a giant cardboard box. And, that the kids collected things like macaroni and cheese, cans of alphabet letters with red sauce, boxes of cereal, and ketchup and mustard. Are these items that can be left in a cardboard box and not refrigerated? So, if these items are nonperishable, then what would nonperishable mean? Why would items in a food drive need to be nonperishable?

Finally, Mary directed students to use the order of the keywords on the chart to write a summary describing the Tree Town Preschool event. While summarizing the events was the goal of this portion, it also provided an opportunity to integrate sequential writing. Using sentence starters with spaces for "First," "Next," and "Finally," students worked independently to create sequential summaries of the text (see figure 6.2). Some of the summaries were very simple. Following are examples:

> *First student brainstormed ideas. Next they decided to collect food. Finally they donated the food.*

Other summaries were more sophisticated.

> *First students brainstormed ways to help their community. Next, they decided to collect and categorize nonperishable food items. Finally, they donated the food items to a local food pantry.*

Although one summary included more keywords and details than the other, they both show a strong grasp of sequential writing and comprehension of the article.

STRUCTURE SORT: Sequence

TEXT TITLE: **Tree Town Preschool Gives Thanks**

KEY WORDS: **decorate, collect, ideas, donate, brainstorm, non-perishable, categorize**

- SORT

FIRST	+ or -	THEN	+ or -	FINALLY	+ or -
1. brainstorm	+	2. collect	+	non-perishable	+ 3.
2. ideas	+	7. donate	–	categorize	+ 6.
		4. decorate	+		

- PREDICT The event might be where they come up with ideas to collect stuff and donate it.

- READ & CHECK (+ or -)

- SUMMARIZE First, the students brainstormed ideas. Next, they decided to collect food. Finally, they donated the food.

Figure 6.2.   Sequence Structure Sort Sample. *Source*: Mary Hoch.

Key Points

- Articles from local newspapers are not only excellent resources for informational text examples, but they also help students engage with their local community and learn about media from an early age.
- Strong, focused predictions can lead to deeper understanding. Begin by activating background knowledge.
- Be sure to spend time helping students use (1) the title, (2) the keywords, and (3) the text structure to produce a strong prediction.
- Use the Read and Check to incorporate stopping points where students monitor their understanding.
- When challenging words are not predefined, be sure to revisit them After Reading.
- When working on the sequence structure, use the summary as an opportunity for students to practice sequential writing.

Chapter 7

Compare and Contrast

> **CHAPTER FOCUS: In this chapter we will focus on choosing and introducing keywords Before Reading and creating strong summaries After Reading.**

When facing a difficult decision, many of us turn to the compare and contrast method to consider how two or more options are alike and different. This side-by-side analysis allows us to draw conclusions and anticipate outcomes in order to make the best possible decision. Since this is such an important skill in real-world decision-making, it is an essential and widely-relied-upon way of structuring written information. The compare and contrast text structure allows authors to use common phrases such as *however, as well as,* and *on the other hand* to signal a side-by-side look at the relationship that exists among two or more things, possibly making this the most easily relatable text structure.

To examine this important text structure more closely, we use a compare and contrast Structure Sort. This will guide students in building an understanding of how two things or ideas are interconnected. This is often done using a Venn diagram, which is an excellent tool for presenting information we want to compare and contrast. However, the goal of this Structure Sort is to take students beyond the Venn diagram, by focusing on keywords that are not only essential to the relationship among the two things or ideas but also essential to overall meaning. An integrated approach such as this will also help students analyze the compare-contrast relationship during all three phases of reading, rather than just after reading, which can result in a deeper understanding of the text and its key ideas. By the way, did you notice any familiar signal words in this paragraph? Can you guess its structure?

Let us take an in-depth look at the compare and contrast Structure Sort, by revisiting Owen's fourth-grade classroom. Owen's reading class is comprised of on- and above-grade-level readers. This Structure Sort was done as a whole group, with fourteen students. Owen has been using Structure Sorts with his students for the past two years. Therefore, he and his class were familiar with the process. For these reasons, we were able to choose an advanced-level expository text, in terms of vocabulary and readability. Further, we felt the topic was extremely relevant and would be of high interest to his students.

KILLER BEES AND HONEY BEES: BEWARE OR BEE AWARE?

In the past year, the movement to save the bee has become increasingly popular thanks to social media, classroom education, and even a discussion on the popular NBC reality series "Shark Tank." But, for many people, rather than seeing bees as something to be saved, bees are viewed as a killer predator that needs to be destroyed. Should we be afraid of bees?

When people think of bees, they usually think of one of two types: the killer bee or the regular honey bee. Both regular honey bees and killer bees pollinate our food crops. In fact, approximately one-third of the food we eat each day is pollinated by bees. The bees' pollination is also vital to growth of woodlands and forests. In addition, they are responsible for the production of seeds, nuts, and berries which are an important food source for wild animals. This makes both types of bees essential for our environment. Although bees are essential to our environment, many people still fear the killer bees.

Contrary to popular belief, the killer bee's stinger is no more poisonous than a honey bee's sting. Both stingers have the same amount of poison, which is only dangerous if you are allergic to the venom. Both killer bees and honey bees will attack when they feel threatened. However, killer bees are much more tenacious. They will continue to chase you for miles, while honey bees will give up after a few "buzzes" in your direction. Killer bees also have larger colonies than regular honey bees, so a swarm of killer bees is much more intimidating than the smaller colony of regular honey bees. A killer bee will also lose its temper much more quickly than a regular honey bee. Just the sound of someone walking nearby can be enough to make the killer bees feel threatened and attack.

Although it is good to beware of beehives that may be filled with killer bees ready to attack, it is more important to be aware of how you can protect the bees and the important role they play in nourishing our environment.

PREPARING FOR A COMPARE AND CONTRAST STRUCTURE SORT

Step One: **Determine the structure of the expository text selection.**

Upon reading the first paragraph, initial thinking might lead us to believe the author is setting up a problem. But, after reading the second paragraph, it becomes evident that, rather, the author is comparing and contrasting two types of bees: the killer bee and the honey bee. We see the signal word *both* used several times in this paragraph, which lets us know the author is citing ways in which the two bees are alike. Likewise, in the third paragraph, we notice the words *contrary* and *however*, clearly signaling their differences. Making note of these signal words helps us confirm that the text is structured in a way that helps the readers better understand the relationship between the two types of bees.

Step Two: **Identify the purpose for reading.**

Owen's purpose in choosing this text was not only to help his students gain understanding about the role of bees in the environment but also to help them clear up misconceptions about the killer bee. This text also included complex sentence structures which provided an opportunity to challenge his high-level readers.

In addition, the text included an interesting combination of tier 2 and tier 3 vocabulary, which could take students slightly beyond their comfort zone and potentially stir up some noteworthy discussion points. Such words could help students connect their background knowledge to the particular context.

Owen's goal was to use the discussion points as opportunities for students to hear differing perspectives on why they sorted in a particular way, allowing them to reason through their choices and refine their thinking.

Since Owen's students were not new to Structure Sorts, he felt this text was a great way to also push their thinking in creating stronger summaries (than in the past) that demonstrated overall understanding of both structure and big ideas.

***Step Three*: Select six to nine keywords from the text directly related to the purpose and key ideas or concepts.**

In considering keywords for this particular group of learners we wanted to choose words that would encourage them to reason through and rationalize their placement decisions in order to help them think critically about the text. Thus, as always, we started with the end in mind, choosing words that related to the bees' similarities as well as their differences.

To exemplify how the bees are alike we chose *pollinate, production, essential, poisonous,* and *venom*. The words *poisonous* and *venom* are particularly good choices for discussing misconceptions about these types of bees. In considering differences we chose *predator, tenacious, intimidating, temper,* and *colonies*. Two particularly interesting choices in this group are *predator* and *colonies*. When thinking about the word *predator* in this text, we wanted students to reason through whether or not the killer bee is more of a predator. *Colonies* is also debatable because both types of bees live in colonies but the size of each is different.

BEFORE READING

"Okay, everyone, today we will be working on a Structure Sort using a fifth text structure, which will help you understand how things are alike and different," announced Owen at the start of the lesson. After introducing the structure, Owen considered the keywords. He decided that his students would likely be capable of using context to understand the meanings of most words, but they might need a bit of predefining for one word: *tenacious*. Owen quickly introduced the word *tenacious* and defined it as *persisting* and *sticking to something you start*. He gave an example of a student being tenacious because they followed through on a difficult assignment. Owen then asked, "What is *tenacious*?" and chose a student to volunteer a response.

This is an excellent example of using teacher judgment and what you know about your students to make determinations about which words might require a bit of scaffolding and which words you want students to define through context as they read. In other words, it is important to use teacher judgment when considering how you will introduce keywords and whether or not it is necessary to predefine them. While predefining keywords is a great way to provide scaffolded support and build background, it is also important to provide students with opportunities to infer meaning on their own. With this said, if a word is too challenging for most or not contextually defined but essential to meaning (which should be the case if you chose it as a keyword), then it might be worthy of predefining. If you choose to predefine a word or words, our recommendation is to keep it simple and follow three quick steps: (1) provide a kid-friendly definition, (2) provide a relevant example, and (3) and do a quick check for understanding. As a point of reference, in Owen's earlier example, this entire exchange took about thirty seconds.

In other cases, a teacher might choose to just read through the words in the keywords box without predefining any. This is also a good option, depending on your students and their needs. The point is, there are no hard-and-fast rules about whether or not to scaffold meaning by providing a definition, as it is highly dependent on your particular group of learners. However, we do recommend that the teacher read the keywords aloud since hearing the words orally and the sequences of sounds involved in their pronunciation can be connected to word meaning when they encounter them in the text.

Since Owen's class was adept at following the Structure Sort approach, next he was able to do only a brief review before beginning:

Before we begin, turn, talk, and review how to do a Structure Sort.

Owen provided his students with one minute to discuss what was expected and the strategy components. He then followed up with,

What are some important things to remember when doing a nonfiction Structure Sort?

One of the most valuable outcomes of this conversation with his students was the understanding that "When you sort, it's okay if you're not right, you just have to make your best guess in where you place the words." And, Owen reemphasized the importance of using this strategy as an opportunity to think about the words in this context more deeply and how they contribute to understanding the text structure.

Owen did the first word, *tenacious*, with his students and they discussed placement of the word. Students were then sent off to work with a partner to sort and predict. After sorting and predicting, Owen pulled the group back together and initiated the first discussion point, where students had opportunities to share their thinking about each word with the group, rationalize their sorting decisions, and refine their thinking based on the perspectives of others they were hearing. At the close of the first discussion point, Owen restated the purpose of the lesson to be sure his students had a clear focus on intended outcomes:

When sorting, how many of you were relying on your background knowledge of bees?

Most of you, right? What if you didn't know what pollen was? Or, what if you didn't know what you know about honey bees and how they pollinate? Do you think your conversation would have been different?

So that's important to pay attention to—it's not so much if we sort correctly, it's to be thinking about how the word fits into this particular text and its structure.

Owen's students were now ready to read and check. As another point of reference, the entire *Before Reading* portion of this lesson lasted for about fourteen minutes.

For organization and management purposes, Owen's students do not receive a copy of the text until after they sort and predict. At that point, they check in with him, he does a quick assessment of their work, and he then gives them a copy of the text. In terms of groupings, Owen's students are working in teams (partnerships or groups of three) throughout the entire process, except during his discussion points, where he pulls the whole group together. These decisions are very intentional and well suited for producing higher quality thinking in relation to the keywords.

DURING READING

Since Owen's class is at an advanced stage of implementing the Structure Sort method and his students are able to decode text without scaffolded support, they are able to work independently for the Read and Check portion of the lesson. Owen sends them off in teams to Read and Check collaboratively. This frees Owen up to listen in on collaborative conversations, confer with teams, and assess for authentic understanding.

Owen's class spends about fifteen minutes on this portion of the lesson.

AFTER READING

After reading and checking their sort, Owen's students continued to work in their teams to write their summary. While each student individually constructed their own summary, Owen's team approach afforded his students further opportunities to bounce ideas off of one another while deciding what's most important.

He then pulled the group back together and asked for individual volunteers to share their summary. During this time, Owen posed excellent prompts to once again hone in on his purpose. Here are a few examples:

- *Now compare your summary to your prediction. Which better represents your understanding?*

- *Which words resulted in the best conversations?*
- *What did you notice happening in your head when the word was used differently in the text than what you initially thought based on your background knowledge?*

About five students shared their summary, with Owen prompting along the way. As a result of this After Reading component, which lasted about nine minutes, his students were able to come together to

- share their thinking, learning, and understanding;
- reflect on the reading processes that occurred during reading and integrated strategy application; and
- synthesize knowledge of the content.

This was reflected in the students' summaries, which were stronger than in the past, which was one of Owen's goals. Three student samples from Owen's class can be found in figure 7.1.

Owen's example embodies a true Gradual Release of Responsibility approach, with more responsibility being released to students over time and across Structure Sorts. The entire Structure Sort lesson took just under forty minutes, which can even be split up across days. What's most important to recognize are the many components of higher-level learning that are being integrated in this short amount of time, making it time well spent!

As a more experienced user of the Structure Sort integrated strategy approach, Owen reflected on the experience in this way:

Now that I've had a chance to practice the Structure Sorts with two different groups of students, I'm starting to get better at choosing keywords that start conversations and debates. There was a lot of opportunity to promote and talk about metacognition with my students as well. Drawing their attention to how their sense of a certain concept differed from their classmates' got them to really think critically about how each keyword might fit in with the structure and topic of the text. Asking a student to explain their placement of a word led to either a debate or text-based conversation. Everyone has different background knowledge, so hearing everyone combine that with the given keywords was interesting. The way my students were approaching vocabulary was enlightening to watch. They were not stopping at just what the word means but pushing through to determine how it was relevant to the topic and structure of the text. In having my students work collaboratively, one of my favorite things to see was what happened when they didn't agree on the placement of each keyword. This really sparked engagement and conversation.

TEXT TITLE: Killer Bees and Honey Bees: Beware or Bee Aware?

KEY WORDS:
tenacious, temper, pollinate, poisonous, colonies, venom, essential, predator, production, intimidating

- SORT

ALIKE	+ or -	DIFFERENT	+ or -
Colonies	+	Tenacious	+
Production	+	Temper	—
Intimidating	+	Pollinate	—
		Poisonous	—
		Venom	—

- PREDICT Honey bees, Essential, Predator are less Tenacious then Killer Bees. Killer Bees are poisonus and inflict venom. They both live in colonies.

- READ & CHECK (+ or -)

- SUMMARIZE A Killer Bee's colonies are bigger than a honey bee's. Both types are responsible for the production of seeds, nuts, and berries. Killer bees have the same amount of poison or venom as honey bees.

Figure 7.1. Compare and Contrast Structure Sort Samples. *Source:* Mary Hoch.

TEXT TITLE: Killer Bees and Honey Bees: Beware or Bee Aware?

KEY WORDS: tenacious ✓, temper ✓, pollinate ✓, poisonous ✓, colonies ✓, venom ✓, essential, predator ✓, production ✓, intimidating

- SORT

ALIKE	+ or -	DIFFERENT	+ or -
Pollinate	+	tenacious	+
colonies	−	temper	+
venom	+	poisonous	−
predators	+	production	−
intimidating	−	essential	−

- PREDICT Killer bees are more (tenacious) and have more of a (temper) than Honey Bees. Killer bees and honey bees both (pollinate). Both bees are (intimidating) to humans.

- READ & CHECK (+ or -)

- SUMMARIZE They both (pollinate), and they are both seen as a (predator). Killer bees and honey bees have the same amount of (poison) in their stings. Killer bees have more of a (temper). Killer bees tend to not give up when they try to sting you, but honey bees will just give up.

Figure 7.1. (Continued)

TEXT TITLE: Killer Bees and Honey Bees: Beware or Bee Aware?

KEY WORDS: tenacious, temper, pollinate, poisonous, colonies, venom, essential, predator, production, intimidating

- SORT   ☆ = words used in prediction

ALIKE	+ or −	DIFFERENT	+ or −
☆ pollinate	+	☆ tenacious	+
☆ colonies	+	temper	−
essentail	+	☆ poisonous	−
production	+	☆ venom	−
☆ intimidating	+	predator	−

- PREDICT Honey Bees are more gentle than Killer Bees they are less tenacious. They don't have venom and there not poisonous. Both of them pollinate and live in colonies. But they are both intimidating.

HB = Honey Bee
KB = Killer Bee

- READ & CHECK (+ or −)

- SUMMARIZE Though HB and KB are very diffrent the have a lot alike. There sting has the same amount of poison and venom. They are both part of the production of how some food is made. But they still differ, like a KB can loose it's temper much more quickly than a HB can.

Figure 7.1. (Continued)

Key Points

- Choosing keywords is one of the most important jobs of the teacher in the Structure Sort method. Consider your purpose and choose words that fit that purpose.
- How keywords are introduced can vary and is highly dependent on the needs of the learners. Teacher judgment is required! It may be necessary to predefine a word or words, while others can be left for figuring out in context. However, we recommend reading all words aloud so that sequences of sound when spoken can be connected to meaning while reading.
- If and when predefining a word or words, be brief and follow three quick steps: (1) provide a kid-friendly definition, (2) provide a relevant example, and (3) do a quick check for understanding.
- Independent application in authentic reading situations is the overarching intended outcome. Utilize a Gradual Release of Responsibility approach and collaborative grouping options to help you get there.

Chapter 8

Cause and Effect

> **CHAPTER FOCUS: In this chapter we will focus on scaffolding in the During Reading stage.**

It could be argued that cause and effect is the most difficult structure when it comes to sorting. As with other structures, there are, of course, signal words that help teachers and students identify this structure, such as *because*, *since*, *as a result*, and *therefore*. The challenge is identifying which keywords are related to the cause and which keywords are related to the effect. This is essential for deepening the understanding of what happened and why it happened. The *cause* is usually an action or event that leads to an intended or unintended outcome, the *effect*. And, as with other structures, in order to have a clear understanding of causal connections in general, our students need to be exposed to such connections in a variety of contexts, both literary and expository. In this chapter, we will explore how a teacher's implementation of the Cause and Effect Structure Sort using a short expository text helped her students gain a better understanding of the causal relationship that was essential to meaning.

To illustrate the power of the Cause and Effect Structure Sort, let's step inside a middle-school classroom. To do this, we turned to Julie, who works on reading interventions with struggling middle-school English learners (ELs). Julie worked closely with us to implement a Cause and Effect Structure Sort with a small group, which consisted of two seventh-grade students and one eighth-grade student using the following short text and a guided reading format.

IS TOO MUCH SCREEN TIME A PROBLEM FOR KIDS?

Ask any of your friends how much time they spend in front of a screen and chances are they will tell you "too much time." A recent survey showed that over 50 percent of teens believe they spend too much time on their smartphones, and they feel it is a "major problem." Smartphones, computers, tablets, televisions, and video games dominate our culture. But is this screen time a bad thing?

Many teachers will tell you that their students struggle to pay attention in class due to not only distractions from their smartphones but also a lower attention span. With smart devices, kids are used to instant entertainment, instant answers, and instant results. Even advertisers know they only have five seconds to get a viewer's attention on a screen. This short attention span makes it difficult for students to engage in school classes.

Scientists have been studying the effects of screen time on the brains of children and revealed several alarming findings. One finding showed that kids who spent more than two hours a day on their screen scored lower on tests of language and thinking. Another finding showed kids who spent more than seven hours a day in front of screens had a premature thinning of the cortex, which is the outer layer of the brain. In addition, despite the constant "connected" nature of screens, many teens report high levels of loneliness and depression.

Next time your smart devices are beeping, buzzing, ringing, or calling your name, think twice before getting behind the screen.

PREPARING FOR A CAUSE AND EFFECT STRUCTURE SORT

Step One: **Determine the structure of the expository text selection.**

In choosing a text that lends itself to the cause and effect structure, we wanted to be sure the middle-school students we would be working with would be engaged and have the opportunity to encounter some of the cause and effect signal words that they were familiar with. Since all the readers in this small group were reading below grade level and struggling with vocabulary, we wanted to be sure we chose a text that was at an appropriate level of difficulty.

In considering the earlier text, at a glance, a teacher might see the title, "Is Too Much Screen Time a Problem for Kids?" and immediately think it was structured for problem and solution. And, after reading the first paragraph, it would still seem to fit that structure since the author is posing a problem in the second sentence. But, as we read on, we notice that the author is not posing solutions to the problem of too much screen time but, rather, provides the reader with possible effects on school life and health. As such, we revise our initial thinking about the structure and consider cause and effect as a possible macrostructure. We also note signal words, such as *due to*, *effects*, and *despite*, which help us confirm our thinking, that the overall macrostructure of this text is a better fit for cause and effect. This example reminds us of the importance of reading through an entire text before deciding upon its macrostructure!

Because this is a topic of interest for middle-school students and it fits the cause and effect macrostructure, we felt it would be a great starting point for helping Julie's students examine cause and effect relationships.

Step Two: Identify the purpose for reading.

Julie's overall goal for her ELs was to help them begin to understand cause and effect relationships by starting with an accessible text that would hold their interest. She also wanted them to encounter tier 2 vocabulary not only to activate their background knowledge but also to assess whether or not they were able to effectively use context to build understanding. This text was suitable for these purposes.

Step Three: Select six to nine keywords from the text directly related to the purpose and key ideas or concepts.

In considering keywords, we, once again, started with the end in mind. We wanted this small group of students to understand how common devices that dominate society are impacting teens. To help them better understand this relationship, we first read through the passage and identified tier 2 words that might be difficult for these students. In the first paragraph, we chose *dominate* because its meaning was essential to understanding that paragraph. The second paragraph pointedly addressed the impact at school so we wanted to choose words that focused on that impact. We chose *devices*, *distractions*, *attention span*, and *engage*. The third paragraph involved effects on the brain, so we chose *depression*. We also chose a tier 3 word, *cortex*, here to be sure we were including new vocabulary slightly beyond their current body of knowledge.

In reviewing our words, we realized that most were related to the effects of too much screen time. We noted that *dominate* and *devices* were our only causes. So we also added *connected* from the third paragraph, which was also related to causes.

After rereading the text again with the keywords in mind, we were confident that these eight words effectively captured the essence of this text. Julie filled in the top of the graphic organizer and was now ready to begin the Structure Sort (see figure 8.1).

Cause & Effect

TEXT TITLE: <u>Is Too Much Screen Time a Problem for Kids?</u>

KEY WORDS: **engage, distractions, devices, cortex, dominate, depression, connected, attention span**

- SORT

CAUSE	+ or -	EFFECT	+ or -

- PREDICT _____

_____

_____

_____

- READ & CHECK (+ or -)
- SUMMARIZE _____

_____

_____

_____

Structure Sorts - Developed by: Dr. Mary Hoch & Dr. Jana McNally (2018)

Figure 8.1. Cause and Effect Structure Sort Sample. *Source*: Mary Hoch.

BEFORE READING

Since Julie's group consisted of middle-school ELs, we realized that extra support and scaffolding would be necessary in order for students to achieve Julie's intended purpose. Julie started by having students review the title of the text and read through each of the eight keywords. In doing this, she also talked about the meaning of each keyword which helped her in two ways: first, it allowed her to assess prior knowledge and, second, it helped to activate students' background knowledge.

Julie then asked students to sort the words according to whether they felt each would be part of the cause or part of the effect and share their thinking about how they sorted the words. Now students were ready to predict. As with many beginning sorts, although their predictions got at the gist, they were one sentence and very basic. For example, one student wrote: *I think it will be about devices that are distractions for kids*; and another wrote: *I predict the story will be about teen attention span*. While both predictions relate to the title and some of the keywords, there is no indication in either prediction as to whether or not they understand what these keywords mean.

Julie then asked the students why they thought she was having them use keywords to predict. The students' responses indicated that they understood that these words would be in the story and this would help them think about what is ahead. Now they were ready to begin reading.

DURING READING

Knowing her students, Julie realized some scaffolding would be necessary during reading. As a first step, she instructed students to read the text and underline any keywords they noticed. Students did this independently, but Julie realized a second read would be required. She instructed students in the following way:

> So, we read it once and underlined any keywords we noticed. Now let's break it down by paragraph. Look back at paragraph one. Reread paragraph one and identify any keywords you came across.

Students reread the short chunk of text and identified the keyword *dominate*. Julie responded as follows:

> Yes, dominate. Let me reread that sentence. "Smartphones, computers, tablets, televisions, and video games dominate our culture." Is that a cause or an effect?

All students in the group were able to identify *dominate* as a cause. When asked how they knew, students were able to convey that it was an action leading to a problem. Julie's response was,

> Right, so dominate means to control or take charge of something, which might lead to the problem of too much screen time. So, if you had dominate in the "Cause" column, put a plus in the box. If you didn't, put a minus, and that's okay.

After a bit more discussion, students were ready to examine paragraph two. Julie continued in the same way. Interestingly, she found that this group of students was more adept at identifying the effects but had a more difficult time reasoning through causes. For example, *engage*, in this context, proved to be discussion-worthy. One student, Carlos, contended that *engaging in class* was an action so it should be part of the cause. Carlos explained, *It's saying that they're distracted by devices so it's hard for them to engage.*
Julie continued:

> Let's reread the sentence "This short attention span makes it difficult for students to engage in school classes." So what is the causing action and what is the result?

By rereading and reframing the cause/effect question, Julie was able to guide the student's thinking about the causal relationship specific to this sentence. However, an equally important revelation came to light based on this student's response. His reasoning indicates two things: first, he was able to understand and clearly state the overall big idea of this paragraph, and, second, he correctly used two keywords to explain this thinking, which indicates he understands their meaning. As explained in chapter 3, this type of outcome is much more valuable than whether or not he was "right" or "wrong" in his sorting.

AFTER READING

After reading, Julie followed the suggested Structure Sort format and had students write a summary using as many keywords as possible. As with their predictions, each student's summary was brief and contained three keywords combined into one sentence. However, their summary sentences indicated an overall understanding of the big idea. For example, one student summarized as follows:

> There are too many kids on their devices and they can't engage at school because the devices are a distraction.

And, another wrote:

This story was about kids being distracted by devices and then having depression because of them.

While these summary sentences are brief and somewhat narrow, they reveal a developing mental capacity to organize information in a way that makes sense, which is the goal of this integrated approach.

Cause & Effect

TEXT TITLE: <u>Is Too Much Screen Time a Problem for Kids?</u>

KEY WORDS: **engage, distractions, devices, cortex, dominate, depression, connected, attention span**

- SORT

CAUSE	+ or -	EFFECT	+ or -
cortex	−	distractions	+
connected	+	devices	✗ −
attention span	−	depression	+
engage	−		
dominate	+		

- PREDICT <u>Its going to be about devices that are distractions.</u>

- READ & CHECK (+ or −)
- SUMMARIZE <u>There are too many kids on their devices and they can't engage at school because the devices are a distraction.</u>

Structure Sorts - Developed by: Dr. Mary Hoch & Dr. Jana McNally (2018)

Figure 8.2. Cause and Effect Structure Sort Student Sample. *Source*: Mary Hoch.

As a result of the Structure Sort integrated strategy approach, Julie was able to clearly identify areas she needed to work on with her students. In reflecting on the lesson, she shared the following ideas:

The keywords are important and next time I would like to pre-teach the words especially because they are EL students. I also would like to spend more time working on predictions and summaries. Some of the students are not strong writers and this can help them learn how to use the new vocabulary words in each of these sections [predicting and summarizing]. *I also would like to create an anchor chart with the keywords so they can see them all year long.*

Key Points

- Be sure to read through an entire text before deciding upon its macrostructure.
- Scaffold where needed! This is essential to supporting ELs and struggling readers at their developmental level. Supporting the process is much more important than adhering to the procedure.
- Determining cause and effect can be difficult. Focus on guiding students in identifying the causal relationships that exist within the text. Ask cause/effect questions that reframe these relationships.
- Understanding the big ideas at both the paragraph and text levels is the goal. Do not get hung up on whether or not sorting each word was correct.
- Take time to include discussion points to understand your students' thinking and help them reason through their sorting decisions. This will inform your next instructional moves.

Closing Thoughts

When implementing Structure Sorts, our favorite feedback comes directly from students. During a recent conversation with Jack, a kindergarten student, Jana asked him what he liked or disliked about using a Structure Sort to help him understand what he was reading. He looked thoughtful for a moment, and then asked her, "I guess what I don't like is that it is cheating, right?"

"Cheating? Why do you think it's cheating?"

"Well because if you tell us the words first then we can guess what it is about and we are usually always right."

Jana smiled, "That's called making predictions and your teacher loves when you use the keywords to make predictions. That is something good readers do!"

"Really?" Jack exclaimed. "Then I guess I like everything about it because it makes it easy to read when you can guess what it's about."

Obviously, it is never that simple. But we love Jack's thoughts on how a Structure Sort can empower readers to better comprehend potentially tricky text.

Teachers know that using strategies before, during, and after reading is essential to building comprehension. Teachers also know that embedding vocabulary instruction, implementing reading strategies (i.e., making predictions), understanding text structure, and writing about what you read is critical to building a strong literacy program. Unfortunately, planning and implementing all of those components in a single lesson can feel daunting and overwhelming to the already beyond-full plates of our educators. The Structure Sort method includes each of those areas of literacy while giving teachers the freedom to focus on the components they know their students need most.

It is our hope that this integrated strategy approach empowers students of all grade levels to comprehend and master all structures of informational text. It is also our hope that this integrated strategy approach empowers teachers to implement the literacy practices they know are best for their students without the overwhelming task of creating and recreating multiple best practice strategies at all stages of reading for each new piece of informational text they introduce. Instead, the Structure Sort integrated approach should give our valued educators the time they need to be fully present with their students as they guide them *before*, *during*, and *after reading* nonfiction text.

When it comes to literacy learning, it is our firm belief that integrating multiple strategies across a text will give teachers and students more bang for their buck. The goal is to support and engage students every step of the way through authentic thinking opportunities. Implementing such practices today leads to *empowerment* to become tomorrow's critical thinkers.

Appendix A

Problem Solution

TEXT TITLE: _____

KEY WORDS:

- **SORT**

PROBLEM	+ or -	SOLUTION	+ or -

- **PREDICT** _____

_____

_____

- **READ & CHECK (+ or –)**
- **SUMMARIZE** _____

_____

_____

Structure Sorts - Developed by: Dr. Mary Hoch & Dr. Jana McNally (2018)

Compare & Contrast

TEXT TITLE: _____

KEY WORDS:

- **SORT**

ALIKE		DIFFERENT	
	+ or –		+ or –

- **PREDICT** _____

_____

_____

_____

- **READ & CHECK** (+ or –)

- **SUMMARIZE** _____

_____

_____

_____

Structure Sorts - Developed by: Dr. Mary Hoch & Dr. Jana McNally (2018)

Appendix A

Cause & Effect

TEXT TITLE: _____

KEY WORDS:

- **SORT**

CAUSE	+ or −	EFFECT	+ or −

- **PREDICT** _____

_____

_____

_____

- **READ & CHECK** (+ or −)
- **SUMMARIZE** _____

_____

_____

_____

Structure Sorts - Developed by: Dr. Mary Hoch & Dr. Jana McNally (2018)

Appendix A

Description

TEXT TITLE: _____

KEY WORDS:

- **SORT**

MAIN IDEA	+ or −	DETAIL	+ or −

- **PREDICT** _____

_____

_____

_____

- **READ & CHECK** (+ or −)

- **SUMMARIZE** _____

_____

_____

_____

Structure Sorts - Developed by: Dr. Mary Hoch & Dr. Jana McNally (2018)

Appendix A

Sequence

TEXT TITLE: _____

KEY WORDS:

- **SORT**

FIRST	+ or –	THEN	+ or –	FINALLY	+ or –

- **PREDICT** _____

_____

_____

_____

- **READ & CHECK (+ or –)**
- **SUMMARIZE** _____

_____

_____

_____

Structure Sorts - Developed by: Dr. Mary Hoch & Dr. Jana McNally (2018)

Appendix B

STRUCTURE SORT: Description
Grade: 2
Source: Stormy Weather (2019, March 1). Retrieved from
https://www.timeforkids.com/g2/stormy-weather-2/

TEXT TITLE: Stormy Weather

KEY WORDS: startling, predict, thunderstorm, powerful, severe, meteorologists, disturbance

- SORT

MAIN IDEA	+ or −	DETAIL	+ or −
thunderstorm		severe	
meteorologists		powerful	
		disturbance	
		predict	
		startling	

- PREDICT _____

_____

_____

_____

- READ & CHECK (+ or −)

- SUMMARIZE _____

_____

_____

_____

Appendix B

STRUCTURE SORT: Problem-Solution
Grade: 5

Source: Kolluru, S. (2019, March 7). *Can We Reverse Global Warming By Turning Carbon Dioxide Back Into Coal?*. Retrieved 2019, March 25, from https://www.dogonews.com/2019/3/7/can-we-reverse-global-warming-by-turning-carbon-dioxide-back-into-coal

TEXT TITLE: Can We Reverse Global Warming By Turning Carbon Dioxide Back Into Coal?

KEY WORDS: catalysts, global warming, carbon dioxide, reduce, accelerate, greenhouse effect, fossil fuels, transforming, conversion

- **SORT**

PROBLEM	+ or −	SOLUTION	+ or −
carbon dioxide		reduce	
fossil fuels		transforming	
greenhouse effect		catalysts	
global warming		accelerate	
		conversion	

- **PREDICT** _____

_____

_____

_____

- **READ & CHECK (+ or −)**

- **SUMMARIZE** _____

_____

_____

_____

Appendix B 87

STRUCTURE SORT: Sequence
Grade: 9

Source: ThoughtCo.com, adapted by Newsela staff (2017, October 17). *The French Revolutionary and Napoleonic Wars*. Retrieved from https://newsela.com/read/lib-french-revolutionary-napoleonic-wars/id/36382/

TEXT TITLE: The French Revolutionary and Napoleonic Wars

KEY WORDS: exiled, coup, coalitions, revolution, restored, exploited, monarchies, surrender, conquered

- SORT

FIRST	+ or −	THEN	+ or −	FINALLY	+ or −
monarchies		coalitions		exiled	
revolution		conquered		restored	
		coup			
		exploited			
		surrender			

- PREDICT _____

_____

_____

- READ & CHECK (+ or −)

- SUMMARIZE _____

_____

_____

_____

STRUCTURE SORT: Compare & Contrast
Grade: 3
Source: Bread Baking Now and Then. (n.d.) Retrieved from
https://www.readworks.org/article/Bread-Baking-Now-and-Then/edf558ce-e4e9-4e1d-826d-9c66d5b798f4#!articleTab:content/

TEXT TITLE: Bread Baking Now and Then

KEY WORDS: irrigate, exported, grain, wheat, flatbread, yeast, processed, carbohydrate, commercial

- **SORT**

ALIKE	+ or −	DIFFERENT	+ or −
carbohydrate		irrigate	
grain		flatbread	
wheat		processed	
yeast		commercial	
		exported	

- **PREDICT**_____

_____

_____

- **READ & CHECK** (+ or −)

- **SUMMARIZE**_____

_____

_____

_____

Appendix B

STRUCTURE SORT: Cause & Effect
Grade: 7
Source: Daley, J. (2019, March 4). *Southern California will soon see another booming superbloom.* Retrieved from https://www.tweentribune.com/article/tween78/southern-california-will-soon-see-another-booming-superbloom/

TEXT TITLE: Southern California Will Soon See Another Booming Superbloom

KEY WORDS: superbloom, germinate, scorched, excess, landscapes, species, drought, ephemeral, circumstances

- SORT

CAUSE	+ or –	EFFECT	+ or –
excess		superbloom	
drought		ephemeral	
scorched		landscapes	
circumstances		germinate	
		species	

- PREDICT_____

_____

_____

- READ & CHECK (+ or –)

- SUMMARIZE_____

_____

_____

_____

Appendix C

THE STRUCTURE SORT METHOD

QUICK STEPS—IMPLEMENTATION GUIDE

- Structure Sorts are a method of implementing an integrated strategy approach that can be used to accompany text structure instruction on the five most commonly used expository text structures: *compare and contrast, cause and effect, problem and solution, description,* and *sequence.*
- This approach combines a unique blend of utilizing the author's chosen *text structure, key vocabulary,* and *essential comprehension strategies* like *predicting* and *summarizing.* In addition, this approach is implemented *before, during,* and *after* reading text to maximize student comprehension. This method is ideal for all students, including struggling readers and English learners.

Structure Sorts follow a strategic four-step process that guides students *before reading (Sort and Predict), during reading (Read and Check),* and *after reading (Summarize).*

Teacher Preparation
- Choose a text or chunk of text that is at an appropriate level and of manageable length
- Determine the structure of the expository text selection
- Identify the purpose for reading
- Select six to nine keywords from the text directly related to the purpose and key ideas or concepts.

Before Reading, the Students

- Read through the keywords and sort them into the categories based on where they *predict* they will fall in the text.

Discussion Point 1: Discuss *why* words were sorted in a particular way

- Write a brief prediction of what they think the text will be about using both the keywords and their knowledge of the text structure.

During Reading, the Students

- Read the text and stop at each of the keywords
- Decide if they agree or disagree with their predicted categorization of the keywords by placing a plus (+) or minus (−) next to each keyword

Discussion Point 2: Discuss *why* their sorting decisions were correct or incorrect based on the text

After Reading, the Students

- Summarize what was read
- Elaborate on their understanding of the text
- Apply their new knowledge

References

Alvermann, D. E. (1981). Compensatory Effect of Graphic Organizers on Descriptive Text. *Journal of Educational Research*, 75(1), 44–48.

Armbruster, B., Anderson, T., & Ostertag, J. (1987). Does Text Structure/Summarization Instruction Facilitate Learning from Expository Text? *Reading Research Quarterly*, 22(3), 331–46. doi:10.2307/747972

Beck, I. L., McKeown, M. G., & Kucan, L. (2013). *Bringing Words to Life: Robust Vocabulary Instruction* (2nd ed.). New York: The Guilford Press.

Blachowicz, C. L. Z. & Ogle, D. (2008). *Reading Comprehension: Strategies for Independent Learners*. New York: The Guilford Press.

Blachowicz, C. L. Z., Ogle, D., Fisher, P., & Watts-Taffe, S. M. (2013). Teaching Academic Vocabulary K-8: Effective Practices across the Curriculum. New York: The Guilford Press.

Black, P. J. & Wiliam, D. (1998). Inside the Black Box: Raising Standards through Classroom Assessment. *Phi Delta Kappan*, 80(2), 139. Retrieved April 22, 2019 from https://nl.idm.oclc.org/login?url=http://search.ebscohost.com/login.aspx?direct=true&db=eue&AN=503564350&site=ehost-live&scope=site.

Cazden, C. B. (2001). *Classroom Discourse—the Language of Teaching and Learning*. Portsmouth, NH: Heinemann.

Curtis, C. P. (1999). *Bud, Not Buddy*. New York: Delacorte Press.

Englert & Hiebert. (1984). Children's Developing Awareness of Text Structures in Expository Materials. *Journal of Educational Psychology*, 76(1), 65–74.

Hall, K. K., Sabey, B., & McClellan, M. (2005). Expository Text Comprehension: Helping Primary-Grade Teachers Use Expository Texts to Full Advantage. *Reading Psychology*, 26(3), 211–34.

Harvey, S. & Goudvis, A. (2017). *Strategies That Work: Teaching Comprehension for Understanding, Engagement, and Building Knowledge, Grades K-8*. Portland, ME: Stenhouse.

Hebert, M., Bohaty, J. J., Nelson, J. R., & Brown, J. (2016). The Effects of Text Structure Instruction on Expository Reading Comprehension: A Meta-Analysis. *Journal of Educational Psychology*, 108(5), 609–29.

Kintsch, W. (1974). *The Representation of Meaning in Memory*. Hillsdale, NJ: Erlbaum.

Meyer, B, J. F. (1975). *The Organization of Prose and Its Effects on Memory*. Amsterdam: North-Holland.

Meyer, B. J. F. (1979). Organizational Patterns in Prose and Their Use in Reading. In M. L. Kamil & A. J. Moe (eds.), *Reading Research: Studies and Applications* (pp. 109–17). Clemson, SC: National Reading Conference.

Meyer, B. J. F. (1987). Following the Author's Top-Level Organization: An Important Skill for Reading Comprehension. In R. J. Tierney, P. L. Anders, & J. Nichols Mitchell (eds.), *Understanding Readers' Understanding: Theory and Practice* (pp. 59–76). Hillsdale, NJ: Erlbaum.

Meyer, B. J. F. & Ray, M. N. (2011). Structure Strategy Interventions: Increasing Reading Comprehension of Expository Text. *International Electronic Journal of Elementary Education*, 4(1), 127–52.

Meyer, B. J. F., Brandt, D. M., & Bluth, G. J. (1980). Use of Top-Level Structure in Text: Key for Reading Comprehension of Ninth-Grade Students. *Reading Research Quarterly*, 16, 72–103.

National Reading Panel. (2000). *Report of the National Reading Panel—Teaching Children to Read: An Evidence-Based Assessment of the Scientific Research Literature on Reading and Its Implications for Reading Instruction*. Washington, DC: National Institute of Child Health and Human Development.

Richgels, D., McGee, L., Lomax, R., & Sheard, C. (1987). Awareness of Four Text Structures: Effects on Recall of Expository Text. *Reading Research Quarterly*, 22(2), 177–96. doi:10.2307/747664

Roehling, J. V., Hebert, M., Nelson, J. R., & Bohaty, J. J. (2017). Text Structure Strategies for Improving Expository Reading Comprehension. *The Reading Teacher*, 71(1), 71–82.

"Scientists Study New Uses for Carbon Dioxide" (July 28, 2016). Retrieved August 15, 2016, from https://newsela.com/read/chemists-pollution-energy/id/20045/.

Vacca, R. T., Vacca, J. L., & Mraz, M. E. (2011). *Content Area Reading: Literacy and Learning across the Curriculum*. Boston, MA: Pearson.

Vygotsky, L. S. (1962). *Thought and Language*. Cambridge, MA: MIT Press.

Vygotsky, L. S. (1978). *Mind in Society: The Development of Higher Psychological Processes*. Cambridge, MA: Harvard University Press.

Wertsch, J. V. (1985). *Cultural, Communication, and Cognition: Vygotskian Perspectives*. Cambridge: Cambridge University Press.

Index

after-reading phase, *12*, *13*; assessment in, 28–29; Cause and Effect Structure Sort, 74–75; Compare and Contrast Structure Sort, 62–66; Description Structure Sort, 37; normative assessment and, 24; problem-solution structure sort, 44–46; Sequence Structure Sort, 52–55; Sort and Predict for, 13; summarize step for, 11–12, 28–29, 37, 54, 74–75; of three reading phases, 24

anchor charts, *18*, 19, *20*; for articles, 17; for lessons, 18; for Structure Sorts, 42

articles, online and newspaper, 3; anchor chart for, 17; for Cause and Effect Structure Sort, 25–26; as expository text, 16; five text structures for, 17; Sequence Structure Sort using, 48; student engagement with, 55

assessment, of students: after-reading phase, 24, 28–29; before-reading phase, 25–26; discussion points for, 24–26; group learning and, 24; instruction driven by, 23; oral comprehension and, 26; predictions and, 25–26, 28; Read and Check and, 25, 28; during reading phase, 27–28; scaffolding for, 26, 28; Structure Sorts and, 24

attention span, 70–74
authentic understanding, 28, 62; graphic organizers and, 24, 30

background knowledge: Compare and Contrast Structure Sort and, 61–62; conversation and, 63; for expository text, 3; reading comprehension boosted by, 41; for text selection, 41, 46; through discussion, 25, 50, 59; of topics, 5

Beck, Isabel L., xiii, 3–4, 33, 41, 59, 75
before-reading phase, 3, 8, *8*, 50; assessment in, 25–26; for Cause and Effect Structure Sort, 73; of Compare and Contrast Structure Sort, 60–62; conversation for, 60–62; Description Structure Sort, 33–35; for Description Structure Sort, 33–35; discussion and, 61–62, 90; for ELs, 73; fourth-grade, 25–26; keywords and, 34; normative assessment and, 24; prediction in, 35; problem-solution structure sort, 41–43; scaffolding for, 60; with Sequence Structure Sort, 50–52; Sort and Predict during, 7, 61–62, 73; Structure Sorts and, 33–34; of three reading phases, 24

Blachowicz, Camille, xiii

Bruce, Sarah, 18–21
Bud, Not Buddy (Curtis), 17

Cause and Effect Structure Sort, 7, 9, 16, *27*, *29*, 72, *81–82*; after-reading phase, 74–75; for articles, 25–26; before-reading phase, 73; for expository text, xii, 4, 69–70; group learning with, 69; identifying reading purpose, 71; keywords for, 7, 9, 71–72; for middle school, *87–88*; preparation for, 70–72; during reading phase, 27–28, 73–74; scaffolding in, 69, 73; text structure for, 70–71
classroom tables, 17–18
Compare and Contrast Structure Sort, *63–65*, *80–81*; after-reading phase, 62–66; background knowledge and, 61–62; before-reading phase, 60–62; decision-making and, 57; for elementary school, *86–87*; for expository text, xii, 4; in fourth-grade setting, 58–64; group learning and, 58–66; identifying reading purpose for, 59; keywords for, 59–60; preparation for, 59–60; Read and Check during, 61–62; as Structure Sort, 57; text selection for, 59; for three reading phases, 57; Venn diagram for, 57
content-area, 1–4
continuous assessment, 24
conversation. *See also* discussion: about content, 13; after Read and Check, 28; background knowledge and, 65–66; before-reading phase, 60–62; while partnering, 26
critical thinking, of students, 7, 10, 46
curriculum, 11, 16, 18, 48. *See also* lessons
Curtis, Paul, 17

decision-making: Compare and Contrast Structure Sort and, 57; oral comprehension and, 24, 26, 35; teacher preparation and, 16

Description Anchor Chart, *18*
Description Structure Sort, *34*, *36*, 37, *80–81*; after-reading phase, 37; before-reading phase, 33–35; for elementary school, *83–84*; for expository text, xii, 4; preparation for, 32–33; Read and Check for, 36; during reading phase of, 35–37; students struggling with, 19; text selection for, 33
descriptive text, 19; key ideas contained in, 31–33; Structure Sorts for, 32, 37; writing and, 19
discussion: after Read and Check, 28, 36; assessment, 24–26; background knowledge through, 25, 50, 59; before-reading phase, 61–62, 90; during reading phase, 72
Drewes, Bonnie, 5, 7, 9
during reading phase, 8–11, *10*, 44; assessment, 27–28; Cause and Effect Structure Sort, 27–28, 73–74; Compare and Contrast Structure Sort, 62; Description Structure Sort, 35–37; discussion, 72; group learning for, 9; normative assessment and, 24; problem-solution structure sort, 44; Read and Check for, 35–37, 52; Sequence Structure Sort, 52; of three reading phases, 24

elementary school, 39; Compare and Contrast Structure Sort for, *86–87*; Description Structure Sort for, *83–84*
emergent learners (ELs): before-reading phase, 73; group learning with, 73–74; identifying reading purpose for, 71; keywords for, 41, 61, 66, 73, 76; kindergarteners as, 40–41; problem-solution text structure for, 41–42; Read and Check for, 44; scaffolding for, 74; Structure Sorts for, 40, 46; text

Index

selection for, 59; vocabulary for, 71
emoji language, 32–37
expository text, xi, xii–xiii, 21; articles as, 16; background knowledge for, 3; Cause and Effect Structure Sort for, xii, 4, 69–70; Compare and Contrast Structure Sort for, xii, 4; Description Structure Sort for, xii, 4; five text structures for, xii, 4; for fourth grade, 58; online resources for, 3; for preschool, 49; problem-solution text structure for, xii, 4, 40; Sequence Structure Sort for, xii, 4, 49; student engagement with, xii–xiii, 2, 13; text structure of, 4, 41, 59, 70–71

fictional stories, 40, 46; problem-solution text structure for, 39; teachers preferring, xi
fifth grade, 5, 16, 18
five guiding factors, teaching, 24–25
five text structures, 5. *See also* Structure Sort; for articles, 17; for expository text, xii, 4; student introduction to, 16
formative assessment, 23–24, 29, 30
fourth grade, 3, 16, 23, 25, 58; expository text for, 58; group learning in, 17
fourth-grade teacher, 23; advanced-level expository text from, 58; before-reading phase, 25–26; Compare and Contrast Structure Sort of, 58–64; expository text from, 58; group learning and, 62; Padlet app used by, 29

Gradual Release of Responsibility approach, 63
graphic organizers, 79–83; authentic understanding and, 24, 30; keywords for, 72; plus and minus system on, 9; for preschool, 48, 50; for Structure Sorts, 5; students and teachers guided by, 24
Gray, Kayla, 47–55

group learning, 7; assessment and, 24; with Cause and Effect Structure Sort, 69; Compare and Contrast Structure Sort and, 58–66; with ELs, 73–74; in fourth grade, 17, 62; problem-solution structure sort for, 40–46; during reading phase, 9; text selection for, 70, 71

Highlighted Main Ideas, *21*
Highlighted Signal Words, *20*
Highlighted Supporting Details, *21*
highlighting text, 37; "less is more" when, 20, 31; for main ideas, 31; for signal words, 20
high school, *85–86*

identifying purpose, for reading, 41, 44, 49, 59–60, 89; Cause and Effect Structure Sort, 71; Compare and Contrast Structure Sort, 59, 62; for ELs, 71; text structure and, 16
Implementation Guide, for Structure Sorts, *89–90*
instructional strategies: Structure Sorts and, 15; for teachers, xiii
Integrated Strategies, xi–xiv

key ideas: for content learning, 4; descriptive text containing, 31–33; for summarize step, 5
Keyword Anchor Chart for Sequence, *53*
keywords, 49, 51, 53–55; Cause and Effect Structure Sort, 7, 9, 71–72; Compare and Contrast Structure Sort, 59–60; for ELs, 41, 61, 66, 73, 76; for graphic organizers, 71; partnering and, 7; predictions and, 5, 49, 77; before reading process and, 25–26, 34; for scaffolding, 60–61; Sequence Structure Sort and, 51; Structure Sorts and, 4–5, 35, 51, 77; students sorting, 7; for summarize step, 14; teachers determining, 66; vocabulary and, 5

killer bees, and honey bees, 58–61
kindergarten: emergent readers in, 40–41; summarize step for, 44–46

Legos, 40–43, 45
"less is more," 20, 31
lessons, 17; anchor chart for, 18; for Structure Sorts, 2
literacy practices, 77–78

macrostructure, of text, 4, 13, 25, 33, 41, 71
main ideas, *21*; highlighting, 31; supporting details *versus,* 19
McNally, Jana, xi–xii, 1–2, 31; problem-solution text structure and, 41–46
middle school, 71–72, 74–76; Cause and Effect Structure Sort for, 69–70, *89–90*; emergent learners (ELs) in, 73; problem-solution structure sort in, *86–87*

nonfiction: problem-solution structure sort for, 39–40, 46; Structure Sorts and, 61; three reading phases with, 78
normative assessment, 24

Online Expository Article Resources, *3*
online resources, 3, 5, 29
oral comprehension, 7, 61; assessment and, 26; decision-making and, 24, 26, 35

pacing chart, 11
Padlet app, *30*; fourth-grade teacher using, 29; student engagement and, 29
Page, Ellen, xi
partnering: conversations while, 26; keywords and, 7; for Sequence Structure Sort, 52; for Sort and Predict step, 61
partner reading, 9, 17

picture books, xi
plus and minus system: on graphic organizers, 9; for reading, 9; writing and, 9
predictions, 47, 51–52, 74; after-reading phase, 13–14, 28; keywords and, 49, 77; before reading, 5, 7, 26, 43, 73, 92; during reading phase, 9; for student assessment, 25–26, 28; text structure and, 55; writing, 7, 26
preparation, 91; for Cause and Effect Structure Sort, 70–72; for Compare and Contrast Structure Sort, 59–60; decision-making and, 16; for Description Structure Sort, 32–33, *34*; for problem-solution structure sort, 40–41; for reading process, 1; for Sequence Structure Sort, 49–50; for Structure Sorts, 2–3, 5, 10–11
preschool, 51–52, 54; expository text for, 49; graphic organizers for, 48, 50; writing in, 48
Problem and Solution Structure Sort Anchor Chart, *42*
problem-solution structure sort, *79–80*; after-reading phase, 44–46; before-reading phase, 41–43; group learning for, 40–46; for middle school, *86–87*; nonfiction and, 39–40, 46; preparation for, 40–41; during reading phase, 44; text selection for, 41
problem-solution text structure, 43; for emergent readers, 41–42; for expository text, xii, 4, 40; for fictional stories, 39; preparation for, 40–41
purpose, 4–5, 13, 33. *See also* identifying purpose

Read and Check, 14, 35, 44, 55, 91; assessment and, 25, 28; Compare and Contrast Structure Sort, 61–62; conversation after, 28; Description Structure Sort, 36; discussion points after, 28, 36; for emergent readers, 44; for reading comprehension, 14, 36; during reading phase, 35–36, 35–37, 52; Sequence Structure Sort, 52; Structure Sorts, xii, 9; for student engagement, 36

reading. *See specific topics*

reading comprehension, xii, 9, 21, 49, 91; background knowledge boosting, 41; Read and Check for, 14, 36; text structure and, 15; three reading phases and, 77; topics for, 46; vocabulary for, 32

reading to learn, xii–xiv

rushing, while reading, 11, 13

scaffolding, as instructional support: for assessment, 26, 28; before-reading phase, 60; in Cause and Effect Structure Sort, 69, 73; for ELs, 76; for explicit instruction, 18, 22; keywords for, 60–61; for writing, 45

screen time, 71, *72*, 74, *75*; attentional span and, 70

second-grade, 31–33

Sequence Structure Sort, 16, 47, *53*, *54*, *83–84*; after-reading phase, 52–55; articles using, 48; before-reading phase, 50–52; for expository text, xii, 4, 49; for high school, *87–88*; keywords and, 51; partnering for, 52; preparation for, 49–50; Read and Check, 52; during reading phase, 52; as Structure Sort, 54; text selection for, 49

sequential writing, 48, 54–55

Shared Summary Writing Sample, *45*

signal words, 19, *20*; highlighting text for, 20; text structure and, 4, 18, 48, 59, 69, 70–71

smart devices, 70–71, 73, 74–75

Sort and Predict step, 14, 91; after-reading phase, 13; before-reading phase, 7, 35, 61–62, 73; keywords and, 5; partnering for, 61; of Structure Sorts, xii; summarize step and, 74

sorting decisions, 26, 28, 76, 92

Stages of Development, 24

Structure Sort Graphic Organizer, 5, 24, 50. *See also* graphic organizers

Structure Sorts, xiii–xiv, 3, 7, 13–15, 24, 28–29; anchor chart for, 42; assessment and, 24; before-reading phase, 33–34; curriculum shaping, 16; for descriptive text, 32, 37; for emergent readers, 40, 46; five guiding factors for, 24–25; instructional strategies and, 15; keywords and, 4–5, 35, 51, 77; lessons for, 2; for nonfiction, 61; preparation for, 2–3, 5, 10–11; sequence method of, 54; for third-grade, 48–50; writing and, 25

Structure Sort Summary Chart, *13*

student engagement, xi; with articles, 55; attentional span challenging, 70; with expository text, xii–xiii, 2, 13; Padlet app and, 29; Read and Check for, 36; smart devices and, 74; summarize step for, 29, 37, 44–46; through active reading, 9

students. *See also* assessment, of students: assessment predictions, 25–26, 28; attention span of, 70–74; authentic understanding and, 24, 28, 30, 62; critical thinking among, 7, 10, 46; description text structure and, 19; five text structures introduced to, 16; graphic organizers guiding, 24; keywords sorted by, 7; text structure, identifying, 16

summarize step, xii, 5, *45*, 55, 89; after-reading phase, 11–12, 28–29, 37, 54, 74–75; keywords for, 14; for kindergarten students, 44–46; Sort and Predict linked with, 76; for student engagement, 29, 37; for writing, 5

supporting details, 19, 20, *21*

Teacher-Prepared Structure Sort, *6*
teachers, 69–74, 76; before-reading phase, 25–26; fictional stories preferred by, xi; fourth-grade, 23, 25–26, 58–64, 62; graphic organizers guiding, 24; instructional strategies for, xiii; keywords determined by, 66; literacy practices implemented by, 77–78; Padlet app used by, 29; text structure and, 4, 15–22
teaching. *See specific topics*
Teaching Text Structure, 15–22
text. *See specific topics*
text selection, 3, 40; background knowledge for, 41, 46; for Compare and Contrast Structure Sort, 59; for Description Structure Sort, 33; for ELs, 59; for group learning, 70, 71; for problem-solution structure sort, 41; for Sequence Structure Sort, 49; text structure and, 70–71, 91; topics for, 3, 40, 46
text structure, xiv, 19, *20*. *See also* five text structures; problem solution text structure; for Cause and Effect Structure Sort, 70–71; explicit instruction for, 18; of expository text, 4, 41, 59, 70–71; identifying purpose and, 16; predictions and, 55; reading comprehension and, 15; signal words and, 4, 18, 48, 59, 69, 70–71; students identifying, 16, 19; teachers and, 4, 15–22; text selection and, 70–71, 91; topic selection and, 65–66

Text Structure Anchor Chart, *20*
Text Structure Signal Words, *4*
"think-aloud" model, 43
third grade, 16, 47–55, 49
three phases, of reading, 2, 24, 29–30. *See also* after-reading phase; before-reading phase; during reading phase; Compare and Contrast Structure Sort for, 57; with nonfiction, 78; reading comprehension and, 77
three-tiered approach, xiii, 3–4, 33, 41, 59, 75
topics of discussion. *See also* text selection: background knowledge of, 5; for reading comprehension, 46; for text selection, 3, 40, 46; text structure and, 65–66
Tree Town Preschool, 48, 51, 54

Venn diagram, 57
vocabulary: for ELs, 71; keywords and, 5; for reading comprehension, 32
Vygoskian principles, 23–24

William, Joan, 17–19
writing: descriptive text and, 19; organization for, 15; plus and minus system in, 9; predictions, 7, 26; in preschool, 48; scaffolding for, 45; as sequential, 48, 54–55; Structure Sorts and, 25; summarize step for, 5

About the Authors

Mary L. Hoch is an assistant professor at National Louis University (NLU) in Chicago, Illinois, where she teaches graduate classes in literacy education. She also is the practicum director and director of The Reading Center for the reading program at NLU. Prior to joining NLU, Mary was a school administrator, a curriculum specialist, a reading teacher, and a classroom teacher at the elementary level. Her entire career in education has been focused on meeting the needs of students experiencing difficulties in literacy. She has published several articles and shares her work on a variety of literacy topics at state and national conferences.

Jana L. McNally has been a classroom teacher, staff developer, and professor of literacy education courses for undergraduate and graduate students. As a middle-school literacy teacher, she continually focused on creating a community of motivated and passionate readers and writers in her classroom. She frequently lectures and shares her work on various topics, including building reading motivation for adolescent males through new literacies. She is an avid reader of children's and adolescent literature and is always eager for book recommendations from elementary and middle-school students.

www.ingramcontent.com/pod-product-compliance
Lightning Source LLC
Chambersburg PA
CBHW051815230426
43672CB00012B/2742